HĀ'ENA

Through the Eyes of the Ancestors

HĀʻENA

Through the Eyes of the Ancestors

Carlos Andrade

A Latitude 20 Book
University of Hawaiʻi Press
Honolulu

PAGE I

Kala Kelau, Hanalei, Kauaʻi, Hawaiʻi, ca. 1920.
Louis R. Sullivan Collection, Bishop Museum.

PAGE II (DETAIL); PAGES XX–XXI

Makaʻāinana—*those that live on the land.* Hoaʻāina *at loʻi complex fronting*
Limahuli Valley. Photograph by Alfred Mitchell, 1892, Bishop Museum.

PAGE IV–V

Bullock riders gather on the coastal plain. Mānoa valley is in the background.
Photograph by Alfred Mitchell, 1892, Bishop Museum.

Publication of this book has been assisted by grants from the
National Tropical Botanical Gardens, Lannan Foundation,
Kamakakūokalani Center for Hawaiian Studies,
and Indigenous Communities Mapping Initiative.

Printed in the United States of America

Paperback edition 2009

14 13 12 11 10 09   7 6 5 4 3 2

Library of Congress Cataloging-in-Publication Data
Andrade, Carlos, 1944–
Haʻena : through the eyes of the ancestors / by Carlos Andrade.
p. cm.
Includes bibliographical references and index.
ISBN 978-0-8248-3119-6 (hardcover : alk. paper)
ISBN 978-0-8248-3410-4 (pbk : alk. paper)
1. Haena (Hawaii)—History. 2. Haena (Hawaii)—Social life and customs.
3. Hawaiians—Hawaii—Haena—Social life and customs. 4. Hawaiians—
Land Tenure—Hawaii—Haena—History. 5. Land tenure—Social aspects—
Hawaii—Haena—History. 6. Human ecology—Hawaii—Haena—History.
7. Kauai (Hawaii)—History. 8. Kauai (Hawaii)—Social life and customs.
9. Haena (Hawaii)—Folklore. 10. Kauai (Hawaii)—Folklore. I. Title.
DU629.H18A53 2008
996.9ʻ1—dc22
2008011337

University of Hawaiʻi Press books are printed on acid-free
paper and meet the guidelines for permanence and
durability of the Council on Library Resources.

Designed by Barbara Pope Book Design

◇◇◇◇

To my father, Lawrence, who told us stories.
To my mother, Angeline, who read us books.
For my children,
Makaliʻi
Pelikaokamanaʻoʻiʻo
Kaimalino
For our moʻopuna
Makaliʻiliʻi
Hoʻoipoikeahemakaniohāliʻimailelauliʻi
Kaleohoneakawaianuheaolimahuli
Kamaliʻiolono
Hāliʻimailelauliʻiliʻi
and my lover, wife, and friend
Maile.

Photograph by Chipper Wichman, 2007.

'Ō'ili pulelo ke ahi o Makana.

◊◊◊◊

Limahuli Garden's restored lo'i. The ones shown are only a fraction of those that still exist. Many, covered today by invasive alien trees and brush, flank the stream on the valley floor, perch on the slopes over the stream, or cover the alluvial plain where the stream meets the sea. Photograph by Piliāmo'o © 2002.

CONTENTS

Hea mai o Makana me he ipo ala

◇◇◇◇

Makana beckons as a sweetheart to a lover

Photograph by Alfred Mitchell, 1892
Bishop Museum

Foreword

Hā'ena, the intense breath of the sun, reverberates through the archipelago, beginning first at the easternmost tip at Hā'ena, Puna, and on to the northwest coast of Hā'ena, Kohala, on the island of Hawai'i. Again, its breath is felt on the northern tip of Kaua'i at Hā'ena, Halele'a. The intense breath of the sun continues to the island of Mokumanamana, where it crosses Ke Ala Polohiwa a Kāne, the dark pathway of Kāne, moving out of our universe and into the spiritual realm of Kāne. *Hā'ena,* defined as intense *hā* (breath), is the sun's exhalation as it first appears in the morning on the eastern horizon and then again at the last expiration of light as it sets in the west. It is the parallel of the first and last breaths of a human.

Kai'aikawaha lists Mokumanamana as Hā'ena, Hā'enakū, Hā'enaa'e, Hā'ena-ala, and Hā'enamoe. As if collaborating with the concept of the intense breath, there at that island is the junction of the sun's pathway. It lingers a little longer than usual before it sinks down into the pit and the night absorbs its brilliance. Upon its return the next day in the east, it has already begun to move south for its journey to Ke Ala Polohiwa a Kanaloa. Hā'ena, the breath of life, a mystery of profound intensity.

Throughout the waves of gods and men arriving on the shores of Hawai'i it is Hā'ena of Kaua'i that gained the greatest reputation for life and living. For the love of a woman, a life is taken, and for the love of a sister, life is restored at Hā'ena. In mythical times, the drums of Kē'ē at Hā'ena lured Wahinekapu from Hā'ena in Puna to Hā'ena of Kaua'i for union with the dancer. It is not so much the drum but the spirit of hula urging *kumu hula* today to travel to Kē'ē, uniting contemporary Hālau with Laka, Hi'iaka, and Pele to be endowed with the primal god forms, images, and sounds of hula.

Hā'ena itself is endowed with potent life-giving energies of the gods. The golden rain against the cliff of Makana, the early morning rainbow that stands with one foot in the ocean and the other at Kē'ē, the abundance of fresh water flowing, *ma uka* to *ma kai,* and the winds slipping through the crevices of the ridges are only some of the images that have spanned lifetimes. The space above Hā'ena is active with birds, rain, evaporation, wind, sun, and rainbows, the earth, fertile soil, and bubbling water, promising life to anything that will grow. The sea is teeming with creatures from the simplest life form to the most complex. And only the most worthy experience Hā'ena from childhood until wrapped in *kapa.*

Pualani Kanahele

Left to right: Halaki Kelau,
Maraea Kelau (child), John
Uo Mahuiki, Kapae Mahuiki,
Joshua Keahi Mahuiki, Hāʻena,
Kauaʻi, Hawaiʻi, February 1921.
Louis R. Sullivan Collection,
Bishop Museum.

Preface

In 1778, Captain Cook ventured into the North Pacific, where he encountered thriving groups of people occupying high islands located almost at the extreme northerly track of the sun. He was amazed by their physical appearance, social organization, and industry. He was even more amazed to find they spoke the same language as people he and his crew had previously encountered almost three thousand miles away in Tahiti. Cook and his men were the vanguard of a flood of European and later American influences affecting all dimensions of life in these islands. The arrival of Captain Cook and others representing predatory nations of Europe and the Americas coursing through the Pacific seeking access to the riches of the East signaled accelerating changes in the natural, economic, political, and social domains in these islands. Later, when the nation of Hawai'i was taken over and occupied by the United States, even more disruptive transformations came over the land, affecting its aboriginal people. Of course, change is the one, ever-present constant wherever one goes in the world or in history, for that matter. The fledgling nation of Hawai'i adapted as best it could to these rapid changes for more than a century. Once deprived of its independence, however, changes for the aboriginal people hastened at an even more rapid pace and continue to do so today.

The stories of Hā'ena contained herein chronicle some of these changes. Hā'ena is only one place in an archipelago filled with storied places. Like many places in the world, Hā'ena is filled with the memories, activities, values, and the spirit of its people. Examples of the perspectives of the indigenous people of Hā'ena can be found in their oral traditions (*mele, 'oli, ka'ao, mo'olelo*), in their dances, and in the meanings of names affixed to the land. These names are attached to rocks, waters, and reefs. They are found in forests, on the peaks of the uplands, in the hollows of the lowlands, far out on the wind-swept sea, and out into the universe of stars overhead. Many are kept alive in the daily activities, spiritual life, and discourse of the few *kanaka maoli* (the aboriginal people) living there today.

People all over the world hold and enjoy visions of Hawai'i. Some of these images are induced by fantasies generated in the movies of Hollywood and on the flickering faces of television sets. Others are generated and fueled by richly subsidized advertisements generated by the Hawai'i Tourist Authority, corporate entities managing chains of resorts, beckoning Web pages of proliferating numbers of vacation rentals, and conversations between travelers sharing experiences after having sojourned there. In little over two centuries, Hawai'i, at the crossroads of the Pacific, has become home to a multiethnic population made up of individuals arriving from both East and West.

Native ways and perceptions, in many instances, have been and continue to be submerged by increasing numbers of newcomers who now own and inhabit the majority of the lands in Hawai'i, greatly outnumbering the aboriginal people. The stories recorded in this narrative of gods, heroes, and villains, of love, passion, and betrayal, of adventure, seduction, and tragedy, are the legacy of those who came to these islands more than two thousand years ago and are evidence of the long association of the aboriginal Hawaiian people with their island homeland.

I wrote this narrative of Hā'ena for several reasons. One was to preserve for the youth of the Native Hawaiian community a record of the legacy inscribed upon the land left by the ancestors. New names and new geographies continue to be draped over the landscape. New perceptions are published in guidebooks, iterated in travelogues, displayed in car rental maps, and passed from one traveler to another. The heritage of the indigenous people is slowly being submerged beneath a growing tide of globalization. The passing of older generations makes the task of collecting, preserving, and publishing the stories of the land and recollections of the elders increasingly important. Younger generations know less and less about their *one hānau* (sands of their birth—a traditional Hawaiian epithet for one's homeland). Compiling this narrative was central to providing a record of what has gone before and continues to be a foundation for today.

The first two chapters of the book explore stories attached to the land. Sources for the stories include oral traditions passed informally over the years from generation to generation as well as a wide variety of books and texts containing stories of Hā'ena. One such source was the archive of thousands of pages of preserved Hawaiian-language newspapers published beginning in the early 1800s and continuing until the early 1900s. The riches in this resource were only just barely tapped.

Another reason for this book is to address the lack of information and the many misconceptions people have about the process through which the land there, traditionally held in common by Native people, came to be fragmented into the private property regime found in effect today. Penetration by nations from Europe and the Americas into the Pacific wrought many changes in the demography, geography, and social structures native to the islands of Oceania. Almost all these island nations have been sliced, diced, and divided between the nations of continental Europe and the Americas. Native people of Oceania rightly feel their homelands been taken through what one Maori writer calls "legal artifice."

In the case of Hawai'i, newcomers, often ignorant of the history of the islands, mistakenly assume the Native people of Hawai'i agreed that their islands should become a part of the United States. Another mistaken assumption of those who only know Hawai'i as the fiftieth U.S. state is that the basic structure of law in the islands concerning land is identical to law in the continental United States. Visitors, more recent immigrants living in Hā'ena, and especially younger generations of islanders both Hawaiian and otherwise need to understand the changes produced by the currents of history.

Thus, the third chapter in this book examines, in a fair amount of detail, the process by which privatization of land came to exist in Hawai'i. The fourth chapter focuses on changes in the structure of landholding specifically as it affected the land in Hā'ena, and how it altered longstanding relationships between the people and this place. I hope that these sections scrutinizing changes in land tenure might offer information that will contribute answers to questions continuing to plague certain sectors of the local population.

S. Kelau and son Kala Kelau, Hanalei, Kaua'i, Hawai'i, ca. 1920. Louis R. Sullivan Collection, Bishop Museum.

Chapter 5 tells the story of a little known part of Hawaiian history. In response to privatization of land as described in chapters 3 and 4, groups of Natives pooled their resources, forming *hui kū'ai 'āina* (cooperatives to buy land). In Hā'ena, one such group purchased the *ahupua'a* (land division) in its entirety. This *hui* held the land as a cooperative beginning in the late 1800s. In spite of an array of coercive governmental policies instituted after the Hawaiian nation was deprived of its independence and absorbed by the United States, the *hui* in Hā'ena managed to remain intact until the 1950s. After more than a decade of litigation initiated by a lawsuit for partitioning the land brought by two *haole* (foreigners), Hā'ena *ahupua'a* was finally fragmented into parcels as they are found on contemporary tax maps today.

Mrs. Kulupepee, Hā'ena, Kaua'i, Hawai'i, ca. 1920. She was the wife of Pa'itulu Kulupepee, the last Hā'ena elder to practice the art of subsistence fishing using traditional watercraft. Louis R. Sullivan Collection, Bishop Museum.

The chapters on changes in land tenure should facilitate a broader understanding of some of the underlying tensions existing in Hawai'i today between the Native people and others. The tension, much denied but often encountered by those who venture beyond the bounds of corporate resort properties and the attendant tourist industry, is often the result of differing perceptions and a fair amount of ignorance of what transpired in the critical years when Hawai'i was a fledgling nation and was taken over by the powerful military, economic, and political forces of the United States.

Finally, the concluding chapter of the book celebrates the lives of elders, some who are no longer with us as well as those still walking among us. These special people, wellsprings of knowledge, humor, wisdom, adaptation, and affection, are living links with ancestors who traveled through the land before us. They are those who, having survived the trials and challenges of time, are living vessels carrying the legacy of those who came before. Like stars guiding voyaging ancestors through the perils of the sea, these special people show the way and enrich lives with the experiences they share.

So, for all of you who embark upon this odyssey through the land of Hā'ena, land of the fire goddess Pele, land of the leaping fire, land standing under the wind watching the sun go to rest in the west, let us venture there and discover what the land itself has to tell us.

Acknowledgments

There are many people who contributed to the birth and development of this book. Thanks first and foremost to the people of Hāʻena, who shared the experiences of their lives and the place they call home.

Thanks to the Hui Makaʻāinana for allowing me to participate in the inner workings of the Hāʻena community in their efforts to keep it a Hawaiian place that will continue to nurture the physical health, spiritual well-being, and identities of current and future generations of Native Hawaiians, both those who call it home and those who visit there.

Thanks to Chipper and Hauʻoli Wichman, who steadfastly supported the many tasks necessary for putting together this book through their work ethic, late evening and early morning conversations, and shared concerns over the continued well-being and vitality of our youth.

Thanks to the National Tropical Botanical Gardens (NTBG) who made possible the Indigenous Communities Mapping Initiative (ICMI) and the subsequent Lannan funding. NTBG and its subsidiary, Limahuli Garden, located in Hāʻena, provided financial support for the book as well as seven years of logistical and programmatic support for the ICMI and Lannan projects. The Garden has championed this work and clearly supports empowering and honoring the indigenous communities.

Thanks to the core team of the Indigenous Communities Mapping Initiative (ICMI), Alvin Warren, Joe Bryan, Jim Enote, and Curtis Berkey, for working so hard to make it possible for the Native communities who were part of the initiative to acquire technical skills and experiences thatwould have otherwise been extremely difficult to obtain.

Thanks also for the financial support provided by the granting consortium of the ICMI, which allowed the freedom and flexibility for the participants of the ICMI—the Santa Clara Pueblo people from New Mexico, the Salish and Kootenay tribes of Montana, and the Chupik people of Chuvak in the Yukon delta, Alaska—to determine their own individual directions, sharing both strengths and challenges. These were the Hewlett, Ford, Lannan, Gerbode, and Tides Foundations.

Thanks to Michael Fischer who championed this work in Hawaiʻi long before the term *ahupuaʻa* was known to the broader philanthropic and resource management community.

Left to right: Robert W. Kahea, Elani Maka, Kuaihelani Maka, Jacob Maka, Hāʻena, Kauaʻi, Hawaiʻi, ca. 1920. Louis R. Sullivan Collection, Bishop Museum.

Thanks to Patrick Lannan, the Lannan Foundation, and Jaune Evans, who went above and beyond the call of duty, believing in Hāʻena and the work being done there. Their funding and encouragement supported both community-building efforts and the ongoing work necessary to bring this book to completion.

Thanks to Jason Achiu and the Hawaiʻi State Archives staff, and to DeSoto Brown and the Bishop Museum Archives staff for their kind assistance in accessing their respective collections.

Thanks to my colleagues at Kamakakūokalani Center for Hawaiian Studies, those who led the way with books of their own and those who supported the work by appreciating the value of what was being documented.

Thanks to Haliʻaaloha Frazier for launching me on my voyage into our *moʻolelo ʻōiwi* by example of scholarly work, her aloha for our *ʻāina* and people, and her own personal dignity.

Thanks to Craig Howes who opened my eyes to the idiosyncrasies of my Hawaiian Creole roots and helped me understand that revising never ends.

Thanks to the mentor/coaches on my dissertation committee for critique, questions, and encouragement to complete the foundation for what was to become this, my first book: Murray Chapman, Jon Goss, Ev Wingert, Lilikalā Kameʻeleihiwa, and Brian Murton, who chaired the committee and assured me that "there is life after the dissertation."

Finally, thanks to Barbara, Maureen, Michelle, and Elizabeth of Barbara Pope Book Design for their expertise and patience with me and for transforming my bumbling efforts into a work of beauty and substance.

History recorded on the land, memorialized in stone.
Photograph by Piliāmoʻo © 2002.

Opposite:
Heaven's view of Hāʻena.
Photograph © Greg Vaughn.

CHAPTER ONE

ORIGINS

 HĀʻENA is a place well deserving of the title *ʻāina momona* —a fertile, rich, fruitful, sweet land of abundant springs and waters flowing from the mountains to the nearby sea. Numerous reefs, inhabited by *heʻe* (octopus), *ula* (lobster), and schools of *nenue* (*Kyphosus bigibbus*), *kala* (unicorn fish), and *manini* (convict tang) fringe white sand beaches. *Āholehole* (*Kuhlia sandvicensis*), *ʻāweoweo* (species of *Priacanthus*), *moi* (threadfin), and *puhi* (eel) dwell in the shadowy caves beneath the sunlit reef flats. Sturdy trees, bamboo, and native shrubs root themselves in the coastal plain, spread into verdant valleys, and climb the *pali* (cliffs) into the clouds. In the cool uplands, fragrant vines, ferns, and grasses cloak the valley walls. Sea birds soar along the cliffs, or nest among the crags, on ledges, or in burrows and caves. Forest birds flit through shifting sunlight and shade from flower to flower, sipping nectar from blossoms found, in some cases, nowhere else in the world. Larger birds haunt the shadowy forest floor, and pass through the sunlit openings, scratching for delicacies turned up under leaf litter and small rocks or pursuing nimble insects among the grasses.

In Hawaiian ways of perceiving the world, Hāʻena is a place situated below the wind, close to the taproot of the earth, where the sun enters the sea at Haleleʻa (House of Pleasure), Kauaʻi o Manokalanipo (Kauaʻi of the legendary Manokalanipo). One translation of the name Hāʻena is "hot breath," a reference to the sun and to the volatile, voluptuous Pele, whose amorous adventures are recorded on the land there. Hāʻena is also where the mountain Makana calls, as if it were a sweetheart. In this book, we answer the call and enter the world of Hāʻena, as seen through the eyes of the ancestors, the *kūpuna* (elders), and their descendants, all of whom inhabit the land today.

THE TIME BEFORE US

The past is a foreign country, they do things differently there. However, it is every-where a land that attracts its fair share of visitors. Hartley 1956: 1, quoted in Basso 1996: 3

It is interesting to note that in Hawaiian, the past is referred to as Ka wā ma mua, "the time in the front or before." Whereas, the future, when thought of at all, is Ka wā ma hope, or "the time which comes after or behind." It is as if the Hawaiian stands firmly in the present with his back to the future, and his eyes fixed upon the past, seeking historical answers for present-day dilemmas. Such an orientation is to the Hawaiian an eminently practical one, for the future is always unknown, whereas the past is rich in glory and knowledge. It also bestows upon us a natural propensity for the study of history. Kameʻeleihiwa 1992: 22–23

One of the best ways to get a better sense of how the original inhabitants of the islands saw Hāʻena is to voyage back, at least for a time, to *ka wā ma mua* (the time before), when the ancestors began to fill this place with their impressions of life. As has happened throughout history and in all places, people connected themselves to the sites they inhabited by naming them. The names, stories, songs, and poetry linked to these places offer glimpses into how the ancestors viewed the world.

When print was introduced to Hawaiʻi by the early explorers and missionaries, the aboriginal people recognized the power inherent in *palapala* (the written word) and eagerly adopted reading and writing. Hawaiian-language newspapers preserve a rich legacy of information about the ancestors. Until recently, this information was difficult to access, but now many hundreds of pages are posted online (at ulukau.org), some of which is searchable by word. Much of the material has not been translated into English. However, a recent resurgence in Hawaiian-language education has resulted in greater numbers of people becoming proficient in the language, which in turn has brought to light more information from these unique writings.

THROUGH THE EYES OF THE ANCESTORS

In the Polynesian past, what was important was not when something happened, but where, how, and in what sequence events occurred. Hawaiian traditions pinpoint places as landing spots of ancestral navigators, as locations where the people emerged into the world, or as arenas in which they lived, fought battles, engaged in love affairs, and buried the dead. These named places were, and still are, considered sacred by the Hawaiian people. They preserve the memories of many generations, forming a repository, a foundation for their identity as a people. The ʻāina (the land and the sea) not only provides food, sustaining physical bodies, but also nurtures the social, cultural, and spiritual senses of the Hawaiian people. Visitors, descendants of those who have arrived from other lands and settled here in the last two hundred years, as well as the descendants of the earliest people who have inhabited this place for more than two millennia—none of these can begin to know the story of Hāʻena without access to the stories told by the ʻāina.

When traveling through the land in the company of those *kūpuna* who live close to land and sea, one can see, hear, and learn about the character of Hāʻena. This often happens in the process of "talking story" while spending time with them. The stories *kūpuna* share link particular places or features of the ʻāina to events or beings from the past, as well as to their own personal experiences of these places. As they pass through the land or venture out onto the sea, *kūpuna* are constantly reminded by everything surrounding them that the past lives in the present. This intimate, constant association between the aboriginal people and ʻāina is the foundation for their physical, mental, and spiritual relationships with the world.

Elizabeth Mahuiki Chandler, known to everyone as Kapeka. Singer of sweet songs and matriarch of a large family. Photograph by Hauʻoli Wichman, 2003.

Like traveling in a time machine, a study of places and their names can be one of the best methods available for looking at our world through the eyes of the ancestors. Despite over two hundred years of occupation by those from other lands, a great number of the names have survived—on maps, in land deeds, on street signs, and in the shared experiences of those *kūpuna* who continue to cherish the treasures passed on by their forebears. Place names are an important ingredient of indigenous prose and poetry and continue to be celebrated in songs composed by the Native people today. Names continue to survive as well through the everyday practices of the people who live and work on the land.

Today, as foreigners arrive in even greater numbers than ever before, more and more alien names are attached to the land. It is essential for the survival of the aboriginal people that the older names not be forgotten. The loss of names and their accompanying stories sever Native peoples from their ancestry, history, and identity, and, in this era of globalization, their legitimate claims to their continuing existence as a unique and distinct people. This chapter seeks to recover a sense of the importance of these names by moving through and viewing the land through the eyes of the ancestors.

The following stories reflect the ancestors' knowledge about their own origins and about those beings who continue to inhabit Hā'ena. Stories about the origins of the Hawaiian people predate by many centuries the arrival of Captain Cook and other European explorers. In their written accounts about the islands and the Native people, these later visitors expressed amazement that people had actually located and inhabited for many centuries these islands in the biggest ocean Europeans had yet encountered without the use of what was considered modern technology at the time. Some of these stories predate even the earliest of European writings.

ABORIGINAL ORIGINS

For many centuries before Europeans named the ocean surrounding these islands the Pacific, adventurous, seafaring people had been living in what was to become known as the Hawaiian archipelago. Stories collected by these early Europeans about the origins of the Hawaiian people were diverse and are still only partially understood by scholars today. One source where the Hawaiian people preserved their own understanding of their origins was in the cosmo-logical genealogy known as the Kumulipo.

> *At the time that turned the heat of the earth,*
> *At the time when the heavens turned and changed,*
> *At the time when the light of the sun was subdued*
> *To cause light to break forth,*
> *At the time of the night of Makalii (winter)*
> *Then began the slime which established the earth,*
> *The source of deepest darkness.*
> *Of the depth of darkness, of the depth of darkness,*
> *Of the darkness of the sun, in the depth of night,*
> *It is night,*
> *So was night born.*
> Queen Lili'uokalani translation, VERSE 1, FIRST ERA

The narrative begins with the birth of the earth out of Pō, the time of eternal darkness, and progresses through many eras, eventually portraying all aspects of the cosmos and all beings inhabiting it. This story celebrates the union of earth mother (Papa) and sky father (Wākea) from which islands are born. Also born was the *kalo* (taro plant), named Hāloanakalaukapalili (Hāloa of the trembling leaf), followed by the earliest human ancestor of the Hawaiian people, Hāloakanaka (Hāloa the human being).

Hāloanakalaukapalili the kalo, *elder sibling and ancestor of the Hawaiian people. Photograph by Chipper Wichman, 2002.*

Kumulipo records the appearance of the nonhuman inhabitants of the earth, beginning with the coral polyp. This diminutive builder of reefs was born in the shallow, warm ocean where sea, sky, and land met to supply the necessary ingredients for life. During this era, the shellfish, the sea cucumber, the small sea urchin, the flat sea urchin, tiny mussels, the clam, the barnacle, the dark sea snail, and the cowry, among others, were also born. Next conceived were a variety of paired beings, each sea inhabitant coupled with a land companion. It was still dark. The water was the womb of the deep, bearing and giving birth to all things.

> *Man by Waiololi, woman by Waiolola,*
> *The Akiaki was born and lived in the sea;*
> *Guarded by the Manienie Akiaki that grew in the forest.*
> *A night of flight by noises*
> *Through a channel; water is life to trees;*
> *So the gods may enter, but not man.*
> Queen Liliʻuokalani translation, VERSE 3, FIRST ERA

As the chant progresses through the many eras, life forms become more complex and inhabit the land as well as the sea. In Kumulipo, all are born rather than created. Humans are kin to all that is the universe; all life forms are interconnected, from the heights of the mountains to the depths of the sea. The responsibilities inherent in all life are also woven into webs of reciprocity. The Hawaiian people perceived then, and continue to be aware of, their familial relationship with all that makes up the world. This relationship is particularly important in relation to the ʻāina.

The term ʻāina is derived from the root word ʻai, broadly translated as "that which feeds" (Handy, Handy, and Pukui 1972: 45). However, the feeding is not limited to just those nutrients necessary for sustaining the physical body, but also includes all that nourishes mind and spirit. Kumulipo speaks about the relationship of humanity to the world in terms of family, ʻāina personifying the elder sibling of both kalo and human.

The Kumulipo is not, however, the only story of origins relevant to the people of Hāʻena. Hāʻena is a land richly inlaid with ancestral memories reaching beyond the borders of historic time and Western logic. Diverse traditions exist speaking of origins for those who are rooted deeply in Hāʻena. Most anthropological, archaeological, and historical accounts of Hawaiʻi assume the first aboriginal people came as voyagers. Hawaiian oral traditions contain many accounts of long-distance voyages from various islands and archipelagoes lying far to the south. However, other stories suggest the Hawaiian people have always been in residence. Accounts gathered in the late 1800s and early 1900s from elders on Kauaʻi propose the earliest inhabitants of Hāʻena might have been there long before voyagers from the south ventured into these northern seas. These people of great antiquity, known as Menehune, are recognized by some as the original people of these islands.

MENEHUNE—THE LITTLE PEOPLE?

However fanciful the Hawaiian belief that in the olden days a large population of Menehune folk lived in the mountains and valleys of Kauaʻi and on occasion did the bidding of the aliʻi, it remained for King Kaumualiʻi's census takers in the early 19th century to register 65 persons as Menehune amongst the 2,000 recorded inhabitants of Wainiha Valley! Luomala, *Menehune of Polynesia.* B. P. Museum Bulletin 203. Honolulu 1951: 12; quoted in Handy, Handy, and Pukui 1972: 405

In contemporary times, storytellers from other lands transformed the Menehune into little people strongly resembling Irish leprechauns or fairies and elves of European forests. The quotation at the beginning of this section, however, indicates that Menehune were real enough to be included in a census taken by the mōʻī (paramount leader), Kaumualiʻi, at the beginning of the nineteenth century.

At the turn of the century, J. A. Akina traveled around the island of Kaua'i. He recorded stories about Menehune, collected from the memories of elders at the time. Traveling through the outlying districts, he recorded stories attached to the rocks and surrounding land. His unpublished manuscript, now in the possession of descendants of an early missionary family, some of whom still maintain residences in Hā'ena, is the basis for much that is known about these mysterious people. The following excerpt recorded in the Native language describes the origin of the Hawaiian Islands as told from the perspective of the Menehune:

> *Ma ka manaoio o na kanaka Hawaii o ka wa kahiko, he hookahi no aina puni ole o keia mau mokupuni o Hawaii nei, Samoa, Lalakoa a hoea loa i Nu Kilani, a komo pu mai paha o Fiji, a aia no hoi he mau aina haahaa a waiho papu mawaena o na mokupuni i olelo ia ae nei; a ua kapa ia keia mau aina apau he hookahi inoa e na Hawaii i ka wa kahiko o "Ka-houpoo-Kane" a o ke kai nui (a moana paha) e hoopuni ana i keia aina puniole o.*
>
> *Ka-houpo-o-Kane, ua kapa aku na Hawaii o ke au kahiko o "Moana-kainui-oō" a i ole ma kekahi olelo ana ae o Moana-nui-kai-oo . . . O na hoomoakaka ana mamua ae nei, he mea hoike wale no ia, i akaka ai ka aina o Ka-houpo-o-Kane i hoomaokiokiia e na hoohuai Pele, a me na Kaia-ka-hinalii i ka wa kahiko a koe ae na kiokio o na mokupuni e ike ia nei o ka Pae Aina o Hawaii, a o ka moana hoi e hoopuni nei i keia mau mokupuni, oia no ka moana Pakipika, a o Moana-nui-kai-oo hoi i ka wa kahiko.*
>
> *A ma ia ano, e akaka pu ai, aole ka lahui kanaka menehune he lahui mai kahi e mai, aka, o kekahi lahui kumu no ia ma ka aina o Kahoupo-o-Kane nei i ka wa kahiko . . . (missing words in manuscript) . . . elua lahui kanaka hou aku mawa . . . (missing words in manuscript) . . . lahui Menehune, oia ka lahuikanaka "Ke-na-mu" ame "Ke-na-wa," ua luku nui ia nae keia mau lahuikanaka, e ka lahui Menehune, ame kekahi alii i hiki mai i Hawaii nei mai Kahiki-ka-paia-haa, a ma kahi olelo ana o Kahikimoe, a oia no o Nu Kilani e ike ia nei i keia wa, o ka inoa o keia alii oia no o Kualu-nui-kini-akua, a hanau mai kana keiki o Kualu-nui-paukumoku-moku, makua o Ola.*
>
> *Ua oleloia ma keia moolelo o ka aina no o Ka-ma-wae-lua-lani nei, a o Kaua'i-a-mano-ka-lani-po i keia wa, oia no ka aina noho o keia mau lahui kanaka ekolu, ka Menehune, Ke-na-mu, Ke-na-wa.*

In ancient times, according to the account of the elders, there was only one landmass extending from Hawai'i far south to Samoa and Rarotonga, including New Zealand and perhaps Fiji. This great land, known as Ka-houpo-o-Kane, was a low land of plains, sparsely interspersed with mountains. The ocean surrounding this land was known as Moana-nui-kai-oo. In the time of the *ali'i* (traditional leader), Hinali'i, a great volcanic cataclysm occurred (Pukui and Elbert 1986: 71). In the aftermath, the ocean inundated the lowlands, causing this land to be cut up and divided by the sea. Today, all that remains of Ka-houpo-o-Kane are the heaped-up rocks (previously mountains on the land of plains) now known as the various archipelagoes of Oceania.

The narrative mentions two peoples, Ke-na-mu and Ke-na-wa, who lived on Kaua'i in those primeval times. According to the account, they were destroyed completely by the Menehune and an *ali'i*, Kualu-nui-kini-akua, who arrived later from Kahiki-ka-paia-haa, also known as Kahiki moe (perhaps Tahiti, or other lands in the south). This *ali'i* was the great-grandfather of Ola; many stories about him are attached to places in the western districts of Kaua'i.

Contained in this excerpt is the ancient name of Kaua'i, Ka-ma-wae-lua-lani, which is not in common use today. This name alludes to the story of god-like, ancestral relatives of the Hawaiian people, Papa (*hānaumoku*—earth mother giving birth to islands) and Wākea (sky father). In the Papa and Wākea story, Papa became disenchanted with Wākea after giving birth to Hawai'i and Maui islands, and left him for another lover, Lua (Beckwith 1970: 302). The child born of this union was O'ahu island. Eventually, Papa returned to Wākea, renewing the relationship, and gave birth to Kaua'i island. *Māwae* means to split or separate. *Lani,* meaning majestic or heavenly, is also an epithet for a royal or high-born person. Thus the ancient name Ka-mawae-lua-lani commemorates the separation of Lua and Papa and Papa's reconciliation with Wākea. This reference to the story of Papa and Wākea embedded in the name Kamawaelualani shows a curious intermingling of traditions. Menehune accounts about themselves allude to the great antiquity of their residence, but the story of the mating of earth mother and sky father, told in other versions throughout Oceania, seems to belong to the more recent traditions of the descendants of voyagers from Kahiki.

Though stories of the Menehune are attached to numerous places located in all the districts of Kaua'i island, and to various places on other Hawaiian islands as well, Hā'ena seems to be the last place where Menehune gathered in large numbers. In the broad, flat lands between the hill Kea'alewalewa and the valley Limahuli, they planted foodstuffs in all of the depressions, hills, ravines, and valleys large and small, close to the bird gathering lands of Kahuku. According to these accounts, the offspring of these plantings still provided food and sustenance for the people of Hā'ena well into historic times. Conversations with the *kupa 'āina* (longtime residents) of Hā'ena reveal that hunters and gatherers continue to enjoy the fruits of these plantings until this day.

The reason given for the gathering of the Menehune in the environs of Hā'ena is that their leader was alarmed by the growing number of his men folk who were living with and having families with women of the people who arrived later as voyagers (we will call them "Hawaiian" women, for purposes of differentiating them). This *aliʻi* feared that intermingling of bloodlines would result in the demise of his people, so he selected Hāʻena as the place to which he would take them preceding a final exodus from Hawaiʻi.

If the Menehune were, as some writers have described them, two feet tall, with bushy hair, distended stomachs, and a guttural language, would Hawaiian women have married them? The physical shrinking of Menehune in stories written in historic times by foreign writers may have more to do with Westerners' imaginations than with the actual physical stature of these people. In any case, Akina says that the two traditions melded together as a result of Menehune men mating with Hawaiian women (and in some cases Hawaiian men coupling with Menehune women). This legacy left a considerable population of mixed-ancestry Menehune/Hawaiian children who passed on, along with their genes, the stories heard from their elders that continue to be told to this day.

Limahuli valley as seen from near the place where the stream enters the sea in the ʻili of Koia. Photograph by Alfred Mitchell, 1892, Bishop Museum.

In Hāʻena, the traditions of Menehune and Hawaiians also converge in other ways. One example is the traditional story about a single rock formation located high on a ridge visible from most places there. The story concerns Po-a-ku, a shiftless, feeble-minded Menehune man who managed to exist by hanging around and receiving handouts. Apparently, he also went into gardens tended by the other Menehune, and took food planted and reserved for their *aliʻi*. He was eventually put to death for these crimes and turned into a stone, which stands there still visible today, buffeted by wind, rain, and clouds. This story, told to successive generations, is perhaps a not-so-subtle object lesson for discouraging shiftlessness and thievery.

This same vertical rock is known as Pōhaku-o-Kāne (stone of Kāne), commemorating the travels of three siblings who arrived in the form of rocks from the faraway lands of Kahiki. These three rock people, two brothers and their sister, arrived at Makua, a sheltered bay located along the coastline of Hāʻena. Exhausted by her travels, the sister, ʻOʻoʻaʻa (fast-rooted one), lay down on the sunlit seabed, where she remains until this day as a companion to the reef Hauwā, satisfied in her resting place there. Her brother, Pōhaku-loa (long rock), climbed up over the fringing reef and started up the sloping talus slope just beyond the sand dunes there. The steep cliffs intimidated him, so he came to rest in a spot beside what has become the paved government highway there today. The second brother, Pōhaku-o-Kāne, was more determined. He tried repeatedly to climb the steep cliff, rolling backwards after every attempt. But the *akua* (god) Kāne, observing the efforts of the persistent brother, reached down and lifted him, placing him on the top of the ridge, where he stands today. It is said that when he falls from his place in the heights, the waters of ocean will rise to greet him and inundate the island.

KĀNE

The *akua*, Kāne is referred to in the Kumulipo as follows:

> Man by Waiololi, woman by Waiolola,
> The Hulu-waena was born and lived in the sea;
> Guarded by the Huluhulu Ieie that grew in the forest.
> A night of flight by noises
> Through a channel; water is life to trees;
> So the gods may enter, but not man.
> A husband of gourd, and yet a god,
> A tendril strengthened by water and grew
> A being, produced by earth and spread,
> Made deafening by the swiftness of Time

*Pōhaku-loa rests in the immediate foreground,
Pōhaku-o-Kāne stands at the peak and on the
ridge sloping to the left, the Piliwale sisters
are frozen in their futile dash from the sun.
Photograph by Piliāmoʻo © 2002.*

> *Of the He'e that lengthened through the night,*
> *That filled and kept on filling*
> *Of filling, until, filled*
> *To filling, 'tis full,*
> *And supported the earth, which held the heaven*
> *On the wing of Time, the night is for Kumulipo (creation),*
> *'Tis night.*
> Queen Lili'uokalani translation, VERSES 14, 15, FIRST ERA

The birth of the climbing pandanus vine, worshiped as an *akua* of forest growth because of its spike of red at the fruiting point, which is a symbol of fertility, leads directly to the advent of "the man with the water gourd," Kāne-i-ka-wai-ola, (Kane of the generative water, represented in gushing spring water). Kāne, one of four primary *akua* in the Hawaiian pantheon of forty thousand, is a fun-loving *akua* known to travel throughout the islands among the people. A leading figure among the great *akua* held sacred by the Hawaiian people when the missionaries arrived from New England, he is the *akua* of procreation and an ancestor of the Hawaiian people. According to the Kumuhonua tradition, Kāne constructed the three worlds: the upper heavens of the *akua,* the lower heaven above the earth, and the earth itself as a garden for humankind (Beckwith 1970: 42). In the Hawaiian way of perceiving the world, east is the direction of Kāne, spoken of as Kealaula a Kāne (the red road of Kāne). The northern limit of the sun's travel (summer solstice) during its seasonal changes is the black shining highway of Kāne, Ke Alanui Polohiwa a Kāne.

Stones known as Pōhaku-o-Kāne also were single stones set up by families at their residences in commemoration of Kāne. Those seeking forgiveness for a wrong committed by someone in the family, or by the family itself, would bring offerings and sacrifices to these stones (Kamakau 1964: 33). In Hā'ena, the presence of Kāne is made more tangible by the vertical rock, Pōhaku-o-Kāne, a stone much too big to have been set up by human beings.

KANALOA

Kāne and his traveling companion Kanaloa are credited with bringing forth many springs found in the islands (Beckwith 1970: 64–66). Wherever these two *akua* stopped to rest, they would prepare a batch of 'awa (a slightly narcotic drink made from the *Piper methysticum* plant) to refresh themselves. If no water was immediately available, they would take their 'ō'ō (digging sticks), plunging them deep into the earth. Fresh water would bubble up from the ground or splash down the cliffs as a result of their efforts. Many springs in Hā'ena were used by the people of olden times. Some are still in use today. Known to some of the residents today is the spring Wai Aloha (love water), where people who want to drink water untainted by the addition of chemicals introduced into the public water supply fill containers with water coming directly out of the stone cliff face there.

In the islands to the south, as in Hawai'i, Kanaloa is closely associated with the ocean. The Hawaiian name for what those informed by European sensibilities call the Tropic of Capricorn is Ke Alanui Polohiwa a Kanaloa (the black shining highway of Kanaloa), demarcating the southern limit of the sun's travels.

In addition to springs, the land of Hā'ena also has freshwater-filled caves. In the islands of Hawai'i, Kanaloa and Kāne are often portrayed as companions traveling together seeking adventure in the world of mortals. In Hā'ena, there are two large caves filled with fresh water. One, located almost at sea level adjacent to the government road, is called Waikanaloa (fresh water of Kanaloa).

Emma Chong Hing Ouye, longtime resident and elder of Hā'ena, related her personal experiences with these caves and the *akua* associated with them:

Emma: You know those two water caves in Hā'ena? You can go from the lower one up to Waikapalae. Waikanaloa is down and you just walk up there. There's a walkway that goes up there from Waikanaloa to Waikapalae. Nobody knows that now, that was long ago. No kapu on those (caves), no harm. Before they used to swim and go up if you knew the route to go up. In Waiakanaloa, they used to swim there too.

And they had a boat where you go from down here go up. I think nobody does that now. Like even that, what is that, Dry Cave? Maniniholo. There's a tunnel over there. You go under there and come out by Maka's place.

Waikanaloa. Today, this storied place is known to most as one of the "wet" caves. Photograph by Piliāmo'o © 2002.

*Pele, Hi`iakaikapoliopele, Kamohoali`i the shark, and the rest of the fire clan.
Painting by Herb Kawainui Kane © 1985.*

PELE

The accounts of the female *akua*, Pele, reveal yet another tradition among the earliest inhabitants of Hāʻena. The Pele epics range across a broad stage in the Pacific, including the islands of Tahiti Nui and Borabora in the Society Islands and encompassing all eight major islands in the Hawaiian archipelago and several of the uninhabited Northwestern Hawaiian Islands. Although her birthplace was in Tahiti Nui, Pele was driven from the islands of her birth by her sister Namakaokahaʻi. She left with other members of her family, including Hiʻiaka-ikapoliopele, her favorite sister, and her shark brother Kamohoaliʻi who accompanied her canoe to these northern waters.

Two chapters of the Pele saga take place in Hāʻena. She first appears there shortly after her arrival in the Hawaiian archipelago from Polapola (Borabora). In one oral tradition of Hāʻena, Pele dug into the earth, looking for a suitable place to set up residence in these islands new to her. For Pele, *akua* of volcanoes, a fire pit is the most natural place to live. In Hāʻena, she excavated three large caves during her search for a home. In the first, a cave called Maniniholo, she found only sand. In the next two places, her digging uncovered only water, resulting in caves known today as Waikapalae and Waikanaloa. Visited by thousands of tourists every year, these distinctive landmarks, lying adjacent to the government highway and therefore easily accessible to *malihini* (strangers) and *kamaʻāina* (old-time residents) alike, bear witness to the continuing presence of Pele in Hāʻena. Similar stories are told about Pele at other places on Kauaʻi and throughout the islands to account for hills, cinder cones, and dormant volcanic craters, as well as caves and other landmarks.

Elizabeth "Kapeka" Mahuiki Chandler, another elder whose family has long resided in Hāʻena, recounted her childhood memories of Pele.

Kapeka: Oh well, when Johnny Reese used to drive the bus. He'd tell us he just dropped Pele off down at Maniniholo. But he has to turn over there and he was going pick us up. I tell you, (we were) makaʻu *(afraid)! Ho!... pau (finished), nobody like go in the night or what. Pele known to frequent the area...(She did) not (frequent) Wainiha so much as Hāʻena. Hāʻena and Kīlauea (a nearby district on Kauaʻi marked by the remains of a big volcanic crater). Yeah, Hāʻena because of Lohiʻau.*

PELE AND LOHIʻAU

The place name Hāʻena occurs in both Kauaʻi and Hawaiʻi island. *Kumu hula* (hula teacher) Pua Kanakaʻole Kanahele links the two places through the rising and setting of the sun (see foreword). Hāʻena on Hawaiʻi island greets the rising sun in the east; Hāʻena on Kauaʻi, one of the westernmost of the major islands in the archipelago, bids it farewell as it travels to the other Hāʻena beyond the horizon. Certainly it is no coincidence that Pele's presence in both places ties them together.

According to tradition, Pele and her sisters descended from their fiery home on the slopes of Mauna Loa for an excursion to the seaside below Kea'au in the *moku* (district) of Puna. After refreshing herself in the sea, Pele decided to take a nap. While in deep slumber, she heard and followed, in her spirit-form, the tantalizing sound of drums and chanting of a hula celebration. During this dream passage, she followed the sound of the drum past the islands between Hawai'i island and Kaua'i, to her eventual liaison with the *ali'i*, Lohi'au, presiding over a celebration.

Arriving at Kaua'i, Pele pursued the sound of the drum to Kē'ē in Hā'ena, where she assumed the *kinolau* (one of many body forms she manifests) of a strikingly beautiful young woman in order to enter into the celebration without being recognized as an *akua* (supernatural being). Though the exact details of their meeting differ, all of the many accounts agree that she captured the people's admiration and entranced the young *ali'i* as he had never been entranced before. In several versions of the story, she exhibited her intimate familiarity with Kaua'i by chanting about different aspects of its storied places. Such allusion to places in oratory and other genres is much admired, and very characteristic of all traditional Hawaiian orature. For example, in an account credited to Hooulumahie-hie and serialized in issues of the Hawaiian-language newspaper *Ka Na'i Aupuni*, edited by Joseph M. Poepoe, from June 1, 1906, to November 30, 1906, Pele recites all of the wind names of Nihoa, an uninhabited island 150 miles west of Ni'ihau. She continues with the winds of Ni'ihau, an island to the west of and within sight of Kaua'i, ending by naming winds for all of the valleys and locales on Kaua'i island, including multiple winds associated with Hā'ena. An example is a wind associated with Limahuli, one of two important valleys located in Hā'ena.

> *He Limahuli ka makani o Hā'ena.*
>
> *(Limahuli is the wind of Hā'ena.)*

Limahuli contains one of two major streams in Hā'ena. Two words, *lima* and *huli*, make up this name. Though several meanings are possible, *lima*, meaning hand, can also be interpreted as to turn or to search. The wind is turbulent in Limahuli, which is made up of three distinct areas. The first, farthest inland section is a high, hanging valley dropping over a steep *pali* (cliff) into the second section, an inner valley, separated from the third, outer section by an intersecting ridgeline. The valley walls are high on both sides, causing the wind entering it to spill over, spinning and tumbling. Swirling wind currents ricochet around inside these three sections of the valley, turning and ruffling the vegetation—like an invisible hand probing slopes and ravines. The chant continues:

He Unukupua ka makani lawe leo
  o Lohiʻauipo i Hāʻena
He Kānaenae ka makani lawe ʻala
  a Lohiʻauipo i Hāʻena,
He Kīlauea ka makani kāʻili aloha
  a Lohiʻauipo i Hāʻena,
He Leoʻikū ka makani lawe aloha
  a Lohiʻauipo i Hāʻena,
He Iponoenoelauaʻe ka makani kiʻi wahine
  a Lohiʻauipo i Hāʻena.

(Unukupua is the wind taking the voice
  of Lohiʻau the sweetheart to Hāʻena.
Kānaenae is the wind carrying the fragrance
  of Lohiʻau the sweetheart in Hāʻena.
Kīlauea is the wind snatching away the love
  of Lohiʻau the sweetheart in Hāʻena.
Leoʻikuwā is the wind taking away the love
  of Lohiʻau the sweetheart in Hāʻena.
Iponoenoelauaʻe is the wind bringing the woman
  of Lohiʻau the sweetheart to Hāʻena.)

These five lines all refer to the *aliʻi* Lohiʻau, who lost his heart to Pele. He died of a broken heart after she departed following three days of passion and love-making. Eventually, he was revived by Hiʻiaka, sister of Pele, who took him back to Hawaiʻi island. Here, he was killed by Pele during an angry fit of jealousy. He was revived once more, but that is another story. The short account shared here is only a brief summary, only the merest skeleton of the epic, which, like the five lines above, displays the holistic nature of a Hawaiian worldview, intermingling humans, plants, winds, and supernatural beings in one seamless vision.

The story of Pele and Lohiʻau also reveals some of the social customs of the Hāʻena people in olden times. The hula celebration at Kēʻē that attracted Pele would most likely have also have drawn many people from nearby and outlying districts as well as visitors from elsewhere on the island much as graduation cele-brations and performing arts events do today. Celebrations at Kēʻē, a famous center for the study of hula arts in pre-Euro-American times, would have attracted sizable crowds.

In addition to the physical demands of performing, chanting, and playing accompanying instruments, the discipline of hula required its practitioners to possess a deep knowledge of genealogy, history, and the cosmology of the

Hawaiian world. Hula practitioners and chanters of note were recognized in Hāʻena well within the memories of living *kūpuna*. Their names, as well as recordings of their voices, can be found in the archives of the Bishop Museum. Two places in Kēʻē especially important to devotees of the hula are Ke Ahu a Laka (the altar of Laka, patron of the hula) and Ka Ulu a Paoa (inspiration of Paoa, close companion of Lohiʻau).

Violet Hashimoto Goto, an elder still actively practicing the arts of *lauhala* weaving and fishing for octopus; her brother Thomas, who, in his seventies, is still actively stalking the fish on the reefs of Hāʻena; and Emma Ouye share their memories:

Violet: I heard those old people talk. That's right. Because when I grew up, my old tūtū *(grandparent generation) were still around. Like* tūtū *Ihilani. And* tūtū *Wahinekeouli (Pā). She was still living when I was a small kid. She couldn't walk, she could only crawl. She had one of her sons,* tūtū *Kila, who used to* ʻoli *(chant), when he was by himself. He used to own a house down here in Hāʻena. Then he moved up right next to us. Some times he came around and I would hear him. They said he was a* kumu hula *too, Kila. He used to* ʻoli.

Emma: Well, there was one (hālau hula *[hula school]) at Kēʻē. Yes, that's where Brown's house was before. Right behind there. They were there. That's where the hula dancers when they graduated they went over there to dance. The rocks. But their platforms over there, they (are) still there, the platforms. Built of rocks, eh? Yes and then sometimes, when I was younger, I used to go down there. And there you could hear chants. Chants repeated. Oh yes.*

Thomas: When they (Hawaiians) go to that hula place, they got to be pure. They no can lie, because if they lie, when they go swim inside there (the channel at Kēʻē), the shark gets them. The shark will get them because they (are) kāpulu *(unclean). Because they broke (the* kapu*). You know, that's how, that's the story that I heard. Maybe they don't make it out through the channel.**

DANGEROUS WOMEN AND SUPERHEROES

Pele and other characters found in her stories are not the only powerful beings inscribed on the land of Hāʻena. The Piliwale sisters are a good example. Their arrival and presence in any land heralded a time of famine. It was their custom to visit the courts of different *aliʻi,* lingering there in luxury until they had eaten

---

*Author's note: Graduates of the hula training were required to swim across this relatively deep and swift flowing channel reputed to be the home of a shark guardian as one of the final rites of passage of that particular school.

*Ke Ahu a Laka, sacred to the hula, lies on the slope in deep shadow overlooking
Kēʻē beach and its challenging channel. Limahuli Garden collection, 2002.*

all of the food in the area. Lohiʻau and his sister, Kahuanui, decided to end the
depredations of these dangerous women. They knew the Piliwale sisters had one
weakness: if the rays of the sun touched them, they would turn to stone. When
the sisters came to Hāʻena, Lohiʻau and Kahuanui, as Hawaiian protocol demands,
invited the sisters to a feast and celebration of the hula that had been prepared
especially for them. Their favorite foods were offered them in great quantities.
These included ʻōpae (freshwater shrimp), hōʻiʻo (edible upland fern shoots),
and wī (freshwater limpets), all still delicacies of the land.

The skilled performers of Kēʻē entertained the sisters in a *hālau*, a large
thatched hall built high up on the ridge above Maniniholo cave especially for
the occasion. They draped the open sides of the house with mats, ostensibly to
protect the participants from the cool night winds. At sunrise, after a night of
revelry when eyelids were heavily burdened by sleep, Kahuanui quickly pulled
up the mats, startling the heavily sated sisters. Sensing the fatal rays of the sun,
they bolted from the party. The two predatory females ran frantically, stumbling
down the precipice toward the cave in order to hide from the deadly effects of
the sun. But the piercing dawn caught the panicked sisters halfway down the
ridge, where they stand to this day.

Piliwale means clinging. *Hoʻopili mea ʻai,* a difficult-to-translate derogatory remark made by Hawaiian speakers today, alludes to people who hang around merely to eat your food or who seem to show up often at mealtime, but are never there when work is necessary or help is needed.

Another story of a dangerous woman is of Kapalae, a *kupua* (a supernatural being possessing several body forms), living in the cave Waikapalae (water of Kapalae) and often appearing in the form of a beautiful woman. She would come to the entrance of the cave every day to comb her long, lustrous, beautiful hair. Here she lured a handsome man beguiled by her very obvious charms to his doom. Today, newcomers have renamed this cave the Blue Room, another example of the renaming happening in Hāʻena and in many other locales in Hawaiʻi as a result of the increasing numbers of non-Hawaiians who now live there. However, the aura of the past still lingers in the memories of the elders, those descendants who still maintain the inherited familial relationship with the land and cherish connections to these ancient places.

Violet: *One thing, in my younger days, I wouldn't dare go swim inside there (Waikapalae). But (it) was clean at that time. Beautiful! You could look down and see only blue, clear. So clear the water was, but then after a while so many people came, they're so* kāpulu *(careless, untidy, unclean)! (They) Throw the beer cans! I hate that, really* kāpulu!

*No, I've read those stories about that (*moʻo*), but they are just little stories. They used to say that they were mermaids that used to sit on the rock, but then even by grandma's place there used to be one* moʻo. *You know some people call the* moʻo *mermaids, but the old folks called them* moʻo.

Now, people think moʻo *are only lizards, but grandma's place had one. Because there was a spring there that had the spring water. Before we had some springs coming out right above the swimming pool. When I was small I used to go there with my dad. My dad used to clean all of Isenberg's property. He used to cut by Warrick's side, right next to where you folks live. My dad used to clean all that. Then we used to come into the lot next to where you folks stay. There was the vee-apple tree over there. We used to come over there. And had all these little springs. The story was that there was a* moʻo *who lived there. But after they had gone, the spring died off.*

HIʻIAKA

Hiʻiakaikapoliopele (Hiʻiaka in the bosom of Pele) is counted as the favorite sister of the several sisters of Pele (all named Hiʻiaka). In one episode of the Pele, Lohiʻau, and Hiʻiaka epic, the Pele tradition intersects with the Menehune tradition in another way. The story appears as part of one of the many adventures during the journey of Hiʻiaka to retrieve Lohiʻau for Pele after his ill-fated tryst with the goddess of fire. The particular event in question occurred at Mahāʻulepū, an area on the southeast of Kauaʻi, where a large rock with a knob-like projection on top called Pakamoi can be found. In the story, Pakamoi, a Hawaiian fisherman, was asked by Hiʻiaka and her female traveling companions for a piece of fish to eat (Akina 1904). The fisherman replied she would receive some fish, if she slept with him. Seeming to accede to his wishes, Hiʻiaka loosened her garment, telling him to prepare himself in the meantime before satisfying his desires.

Hiʻiaka told the fisherman she would wait for him atop a large rock upon which she proceeded to climb. But as Pakamoi ascended the rock and prepared to claim his prize, "ʻaʻohe i kau pono iho ka waʻa i ke aki" (before the canoe could be set in its cradle), Hiʻiaka opened wide her garment, and the fisherman was immediately turned to stone. He remains there, a cautionary memorial to the consequences of rude and lascivious behavior toward defenseless and seemingly helpless women, a reminder to succeeding generations to be respectful, even to strangers, as they could very well be especially powerful.

In another version of the story regarding the origins of this rock, Pakamoi is someone put to death by his fellow Menehune and turned into stone for stealing edible gourds from the gardens of Hawaiian people in area. Stealing food or the fruits of another's labor was not to be countenanced under any circumstances. Justice was meted out to those who did mischief to plantings of their own as well as to those of other people.

VALUES BOUND IN FLESH, BONE, AND STONE

Three geographic features in Hā ʻena are named after kānaka Hawaiʻi (Hawaiian people) turned to stone by Menehune for stealing food. Keaʻalewalewa, a thief and mischief-maker, stands as a peak forming part of the boundary between Wainiha, a neighboring district, and Hāʻena. Naenae and her husband Kaʻiwikuʻi are also both memorialized in stone in that area. Naenae means short of breath. Menehune caught her first during a pursuit directed at both her and her husband, most likely because of this physical shortcoming. Transformed into a triangular furrowed stone at the head of Limahuli valley, she was shortly thereafter joined by her husband in the same fate. The stronger Kaʻiwikuʻi, an expert in the bone-breaking Hawaiian martial art of lua, caught later in the chase, put up quite a fight when captured by his pursuers. They crushed his skull and broke his bones, transforming him into a rock described as a pōhaku winiwini (sharp rock) in the chronicles.

These stories hint at what the traditional values of the people in Hāʻena might have been. Those who lacked a means of exchange, those who would not provide their own food, and those who clung to others for support were looked upon unfavorably, and people who actually plundered gardens and plantings of others were often dealt with severely, as evidenced by the fates of Keʻaʻalewalewa, Nae-nae, Kaʻiwikuʻi, and Pakamoi. Memorialized in stone, these stories constantly remind emerging generations of Hāʻena people about the negative consequences of laziness, rude behavior, and stealing from one another.

Kapeka: Hāʻena was one ahupuaʻa. Yeah, and then whoever lived over there, you fish there. Wainiha was one (ahupuaʻa), and then Hanalei. So we never went beyond Hāʻena. The fish (we ate) came all from down here. Only Hāʻena. My father never went beyond his place. But others come. Hanalei people and Wainiha people come to our place for hukilau *(a method of surrounding fish with nets). We, however, just stay our area.*

You know I think if the people of yesteryear were living, oh, things would be very different. Because they know what was proper behavior when you live in an ahupuaʻa. *That is the only way you can go. Nobody else would come in to fish without permission. Because the resources of the area is for the families all in that area. The parents of those days, they no talk nothing. They taught by example. Cause they only work, work, work. Work is necessary to take care of their family. Work in the taro patch, work fishing, work at home. Go down to the ocean to catch fish, come back with fish. The ocean was very important for all the families, because that's where they get their food, eh?*

Traditional Hawaiian perceptions of the world do not separate the supernatural from the natural. The Hawaiian world is a seamless place, in which some leaders are often looked upon or given status as godly beings, dwelling among the people and caring for them, as is appropriate for those gifted with more *mana*, a sign and manifestation of spiritual as well as physical and mental power.

Violet: But you know, when you think about it, during that time those things did happen. The people then had the power. During my dad's day, when he was living here with all those old people, he said there were people who had special power. He said (that when) the person died, the person would be dead for one week, but no decomposition took place. That's when the spirit went someplace holoholo *(traveling).*

But then you got to get the prayers and you got to find the person who could pray to bring them back, to put him back in the body. My dad said that it did happen, he did see that when he was living among these people. It did happen. They had that kind of power. They could call the people, the healing gods. That's what they call kahea *(a method by which certain people were able to heal with only the call of their voice). But they had names and each little thing they said had its own prayer. But they don't give out the prayers (to just anyone). For them it's sacred. But now days, we don't. We don't have that ability.*

Traditional Hawaiians believe that natural phenomena as wind, clouds, sea, and sky are physical manifestations of beings dwelling upon the earth for much longer than *kānaka* (humans). *Akua* and *'aumakua* (ancestral guardians) often assume plant and animal forms on the land and in the sea when encountering humans. *'Aumakua,* deified ancestors who warn and reprimand family members in dreams, visions, and calls, often take the form of living animals, owls, lizards, or sharks, watching over and assisting family members. Stories of the ongoing relationship between Hawaiians and their ancestral guardians can be found in accounts recorded in the Hawaiian-language newspapers and in the experiences of those living who remain sensitive to what takes place in the natural world around us.

Thomas: I never did get chased by the shark. I come down here at two o'clock in the morning, to go look (for) the nenue *(chub fish, also known as rudder or pilot fish [*Kyphosus bigibbus, K. vaigiensis*]). You know, I had the net and the (already caught) fish with me, coming in. I was never bothered by the shark. Some other people are not so lucky. But you see, like my dad, he's a fisherman, his* 'aumakua *is the shark. So, might be that's the way it is. They don't bother their own. Like (for) some of people, it (the* 'aumakua) *is either the* pueo *(owl) or like for us, the shark is the* 'aumakua. *And I guess most of the Hawaiians you know, whether they were fishermen or not, they had* 'aumakua.

Nancy: We were staying with my uncle Kelau, cause he was one of the Hawaiians on my papa's side, Kelau, that's his last name. According to our tūtū *(grandmother) Wahinekeouli, he comes from the* mo'o *(lizard) side, and my papa comes from the shark side.*

The earliest ancestors of the Hā'ena people were Papa and Wākea, the earth mother and the sky father. The *kini akua* (multitude of gods), the *kalo* plant, and the plant, animal, and other natural forms of *'aumakua* are all family relations to the Hawaiian people. All are still evident in Hā'ena, and in the recollections of the *kūpuna* who walk among us.

Thomas: My parents would always remind us, respect. That's why all the old kūpuna *we call them grandma or grandpa, you know, never by their name. You've got to aloha because that's the way. So thereafter you know while you're growing up you're thinking about this. That was the guideline already. That was the way of life.*

Makana, the gift.
ʻĀina momona,
sweet, fertile land.
Photograph by
Alfred Mitchell, 1892.
Bishop Museum.

CHAPTER TWO

HOAʻĀINA, THE LAND AS COMPANION

THE FAMILIAL RELATIONSHIPS established by the Papa and Wākea story place human beings as the younger siblings of the *kalo* (taro plant) and the *ʻāina* (islands) in the family of life. These relationships carry with them responsibilities and examples for proper behavior. The *ʻāina* is the eldest sibling, and therefore responsible for protecting and feeding the younger ones. As younger siblings, Hawaiian people inherit a *kuleana* (responsibility) to *mālama* (keep, obey, pay heed to, care for) *ʻāina* and *kalo*. These primary values set a course for the system of living patterns developed by the ancestors. A brief description of the traditional system of living that evolved through the many centuries of living on islands by the generations coming before us enables us to understand more clearly the relationships between ancestors and *ʻāina*. Becoming familiar with Hawaiian-language terminology and visualizing how Hāʻena is situated geographically within the Hawaiian Islands are essential for understanding the ancestral relationship to place.

SPEAKING OF THE LAND

Mokupuni (*moku*, to be cut off, and *puni*, to be surrounded) is the word for island (Malo [1898] 1951: 16, Kamakau 1976: 7). The widest of eight channels in the group of the Hawaiian Islands separates Kauaʻi *mokupuni* from the rest of the major islands. Most of the time, Kauaʻi cannot even be seen from Oʻahu, its neighbor to the southeast. Because it lies leeward of the rest of the chain, travelers from Kauaʻi in centuries past had to contend with pushing against the force of the prevailing northeasterly trade winds throughout most of the year when trying to reach Oʻahu and the other windward islands. Roughly eighty miles separate the closest point on Kauaʻi from the closest point on Oʻahu. Traveling into the teeth of the wind was a commitment most would not attempt except out of sheer necessity unless they were chiefs having access to large *waʻa* (canoes) and powerful paddlers. Others would probably have waited for seasonal changes in prevailing weather patterns, bringing winds from more favorable directions in order to make the journey easier and safer.

Separation caused by distance and adverse traveling conditions caused Kauaʻi to develop somewhat differently from the windward islands. One example of this difference is the dialectic use of *T* in place of *K* in versions of the Hawaiian language spoken on Kauaʻi in traditional times. This dialectic difference is still evident in the daily language used by the people of Niʻihau island, situated about fourteen miles west of Kauaʻi. Here, the last Native-speaking community of the Hawaiian language in the entire world survives today. The use of the *T* also appears in the daily conversations of some old folks and in a number of place names in Hāʻena, a vestige of the close relationship enjoyed in past centuries by people of those two places.

William Ellis, a missionary who visited Hawaiʻi in the early 1800s, wrote that the word *Tau-ai* (*Kauai*) means to light upon or to dry in the sun. He had heard that the name of the island could possibly have referred to long droughts occurring there, or to the large pieces of timber that occasionally washed upon the eastern shores of Kauaʻi. He further pointed out that the correct pronunciation of Tau-ai is "Tow-i" or "Tow-eye" (quoted in Wichman 1998: 173).

When using the name of the island today, most contemporary island residents use a word sounding like "Cow-eye." When saying the name of the island, Native speakers of Niʻihau invariably say "Kauaʻi": the *ʻokina* (glottal stop) between the second *a* and the *i* is definitely audible. The main reason for the mispronunciation of Hawaiian words today is that very few people speak the Hawaiian language. Speakers of Hawaiian are very particular about pronunciation as many Hawaiian words, though spelled the same, have several meanings depending on subtle variations of sound. Modern teachers of the Hawaiian language classify the *ʻokina* as a consonant, marking the absence of a consonant found in other Polynesian languages. An example is *ʻoe*, the Hawaiian word for *you*. In the Cook Islands, in New Zealand among the Maori, and in parts of the Tuamotu Archipelago, the word for *you* is *koe*. Another example is their word for Hawaiʻi, spelled and pronounced *Hawaiki*. The letter *k* used in those southern versions of the language disappears in Hawaiian to be replaced by the *ʻokina*. *Naʻu* means for me; *nau,* for you. Another symbol, the *kahakō,* extending the sound of vowels, similarly affects pronunciation and meaning. *Kala* means forgive; *kālā,* dollar or money. This characteristic of the Hawaiian language presents uncounted opportunities for misunderstandings when the language is mispronounced.

A well-known saying among Hawaiians is "I ka ʻōlelo, ke ola, i ka ʻōlelo, ka make" (In the word/language is life, in the word/language is death). The belief is that the power of language can produce life or cause death. Correct pronunciation, in the belief system of the ancestors, is literally a life-and-death concern, words literally having the power to send people to their death or to bring them back to health.

KAUAʻI O MANOKALANIPO

Songs, stories, and oratory link Kauaʻi to Manokalanipo, paramount *aliʻi* (traditional leader) of the island in the distant past. Components of his name contain a range of meanings. *Manō* refers to a shark, strong warrior, or passionate lover— all traits appropriate for an *aliʻi*. *Ka lani* refers to the heavens, or figuratively to an *aliʻi* of exalted lineage. *Pō* refers to night or darkness and cosmologically to the void out of which all life emerges, the realm of the gods, and place to which all souls return after death (Pukui and Elbert 1986).

The phrase "Kauaʻi o Manokalanipo" is often heard in songs, as in the first verse of "Kauaʻi Beauty" composed by Henry Waiau:

> *Hanohano Kauaʻi o Manokalanipo, kihapai pua ʻala, ua kaulana.*
>
> *(Magnificent Kauaʻi of Manokalanipo, fragrant flower garden,*
>   *celebrated place.)*

An *aliʻi* of great antiquity, Manokalanipo is remembered as reigning during a "Golden Age" of Kauaʻi. His reign as *aliʻi nui* (paramount leader) was a time of peace and prosperity, for during this time large areas on the island were opened to agriculture. He is also credited with initiating a system of classifying and organizing lands into different categories in order to better manage resources and people. Two of the larger categories within the boundaries of a *mokupuni* were the *moku o loko* and the *ahupuaʻa*. Most large *mokupuni* in the archipelago are divided up into *moku o loko* (districts within). Often, only the term *moku* is used, the assumption being that most people familiar with the land will know the districts within the island are being referenced. The five *moku* on Kauaʻi are Koʻolau, Puna, Kona, Nā Pali, and Haleleʻa.

Moku named Koʻolau can be found on several other Hawaiian islands. Koʻolau are situated on the windward side of the island, usually facing the Moaʻe, the prevailing northeasterly wind. Koʻolau is a Hawaiian transliteration of Tokelau, the name of an island far to the south. This is a name used elsewhere in Polynesia to reference the direction of prevailing winds. Kona, a name for districts found on neighboring Hawaiian islands as well, faces southwest on most. *Moku* of this name face the general direction of the archipelago of Tonga (another Polynesian transliteration), an area to the southwest some anthropologists say is the cultural homeland of the Polynesian people.

Another district name shared by other islands is Puna. On Kauaʻi the *moku* of Puna faces east. This name is the namesake of an *aliʻi* whose daughters married Mōʻīkeha, a voyager celebrated in the orature of Hawaiʻi who traversed the seaways connecting the southern islands known today as the Society Islands to

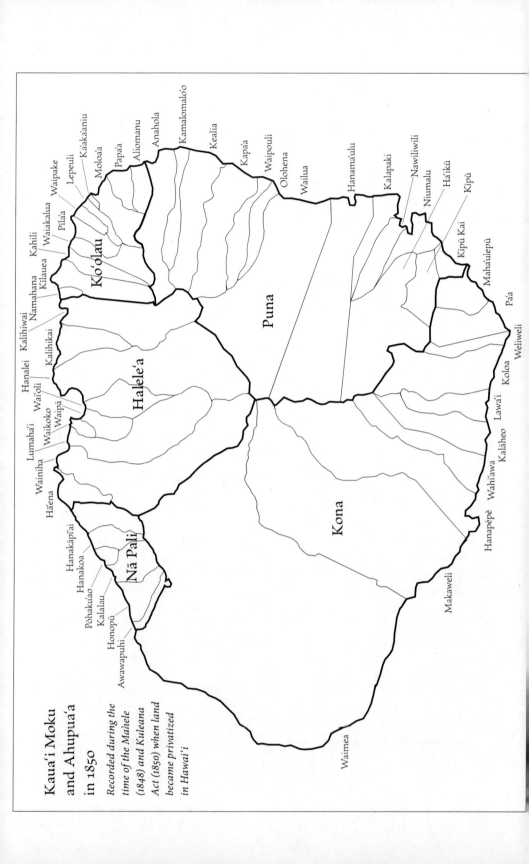

Kaua'i Moku and Ahupua'a in 1850

Recorded during the time of the Māhele (1848) and Kuleana Act (1850) when land became privatized in Hawai'i

Nā Pali

Ko'olau

Halele'a

Puna

Kona

Hā'ena
Wainiha
Lumaha'i
Hanalei
Waikoko
Wai'oli
Waipā
Kalihikai
Kalihiwai
Namahana
Kīlauea
Kahili
Waiakalua
Pila'a
Lepeuli
Kā'aka'aniu
Moloa'a
Papa'a
Aliomanu
Anahola
Kamalomalo'o
Kealia
Kapa'a
Waipouli
Olohena
Wailua
Hanamā'ulu
Kalapaki
Nāwiliwili
Niumalu
Ha'ikū
Kīpū
Kīpū Kai
Mahā'ulepū
Pā'ā
Weliweli
Koloa
Lawa'i
Kalāheo
Wahī'awa
Hanapēpē
Makaweli
Waimea

Hanakāpī'ai
Hanakoa
Pōhakuao
Kalalau
Honopū
Awawapuhi

Kauaʻi. Puna also references a connection to an older land, the Punaauia district in Tahiti, much as New York in the continental United States references Yorkshire in England.

The *moku* of Nā Pali (The Cliffs) is a small district facing northwest and named for its rugged coastline of spectacular sea cliffs and hanging valleys. This name is shared by no other *moku* in the Hawaiian Islands. Like Nā Pali, the name of the final *moku*, Haleleʻa, is unique to Kauaʻi. *Hale* means house. *Leʻa*, translated by some as joy, refers to all the pleasures of life, often with a special allusion to sexual pleasure. A place of great beauty and abundant resources, Haleleʻa is probably the most well-watered district on Kauaʻi. In this *moku* characterized by many streams and rivers concentrated in a small area, mountains are close to the sea and several of its valleys reach deep into the interior of the island. Productive reefs and several sheltered bays provide landing places and safe harbors for canoes, providing easy access to the abundant ocean resources present in those waters. During winter months, waves generated by distant storms transform surfing breaks of Haleleʻa into a playground for *aliʻi* and *makaʻāinana* (people on the land) alike.

Today, Haleleʻa, true to its name, attracts increasing numbers of people to its verdant shores, including the rich and famous from the world over. People from the continents and the rest of the world now spend millions to buy property, fueling tremendous increases in the prices of land and making Haleleʻa one of the most expensive places to live in all of Hawaiʻi today.

AHUPUAʻA

Each *moku* (*o loko*) is further subdivided into smaller land sections called *ahupuaʻa*. The name is an allusion to the *akua* Lono, patron of agriculture and peace. Pukui and Elbert define *ahupuaʻa* as a "land division usually extending from the uplands to the sea, so called because the boundary was marked by a heap (*ahu*) of stones surmounted by an image of a pig (*puaʻa*), or because a pig or other tribute was laid on the altar as tax to the chief. The landlord or owner of an *ahupuaʻa* might be a *konohiki*" (*Hawaiian Dictionary Revised and Enlarged Edition* 1986).

An ideal *ahupuaʻa* extended from the cool, moist uplands, down across the alluvial and coastal plains, out into ocean waters, encompassing fringing reefs and sand-bordered bays. Hāʻena is the westernmost of seven *ahupuaʻa* in the *moku* of Haleleʻa, bounded on the west by the Nā Pali *ahupuaʻa* of Hanakāpīʻai (bay of preserving food by sprinkling salt) and on the east by the *ahupuaʻa* of Wainiha (hostile waters). The *ahupuaʻa* was only one facet of a sophisticated land classification system developed out of a desire to create order, encourage peace, and support prosperity. Historic and traditional records provide enough examples of conflict and times of warfare when resources became scarce to inform us that the system was not 100 percent perfect. However, this system certainly made administering the land easier by clarifying resource use and designating responsibilities among the different groups of people living on the islands. The traditional system was so practical and efficient that present-day resource management regimes are seriously looking to what is now called the *ahupuaʻa* system as an example of a management system much more suited for the integration needed today for successfully protecting and managing cultural and natural resources in the islands.

Although a small *ahupuaʻa*, Hāʻena was well endowed with natural resources. Extending from uplands to coastal plain, it descended from cloud-shrouded peaks broadening out to include a fishery encompassing several large reefs and bays fronting the *ahupuaʻa*. All *ahupuaʻa* in Haleleʻa were endowed with well-defined fisheries, the ocean side boundaries of which were demarked by the outer edge of fringing reefs. If no fringing reef was present, the boundary of the fishery would lie approximately a mile from the beach and encompass all of the area shoreward, often areas where spawning aggregations of different species of fish occur seasonally.

Ahupuaʻa life was distinguished by shared use of land and resources, regulated jointly by *konohiki* (head administrators) and *makaʻāinana* (the people living on the land). The resulting system included *kapu*, unwritten rules governing the behavior of people. Just prior to and during legislation known as the Mahele (1848) and the Kuleana Act (1850) was the period of history when traditional customs and practices of the Hawaiian nation were codified into law. In the new laws and newly drafted Constitution, Kamehameha III, executive head of the Hawaiian nation, attempted to protect and preserve in the institution of the judiciary the life ways that had served the Hawaiian people well for many hundreds of years.

Definitions of fishery boundaries were among many traditional practices and perspectives codified in the laws. At the same time, new concepts of private property introduced by the foreigners (missionaries and other advisors) were also incorporated into the body of laws enacted during this period when the fledgling Hawaiian nation came into being.

Rights to fish in individual fisheries attached to *ahupuaʻa* were very important to the *makaʻāinana*. For hundreds of years, unwritten rules passed an ethic of conservation from generation to generation. These inshore areas, the *ahupuaʻa* fisheries, rather than being perceived as open range free to being plundered and accessible to all, were cared for as if they were extensions of the gardens filling coastal plains, stream-lined valleys, and forest clearings in the uplands. Testimony of elders stresses the importance of the land and ocean resources.

Kapeka: Oh yeah, all of us got to go taro patch. When you big, old enough, everybody go. Because the parents going, they not going leave their kids at home. Everybody go. And then you help fix your room then grandma is cooking already. Get ready for eat. Check the house if all cleaned. When all that is done, off we're going

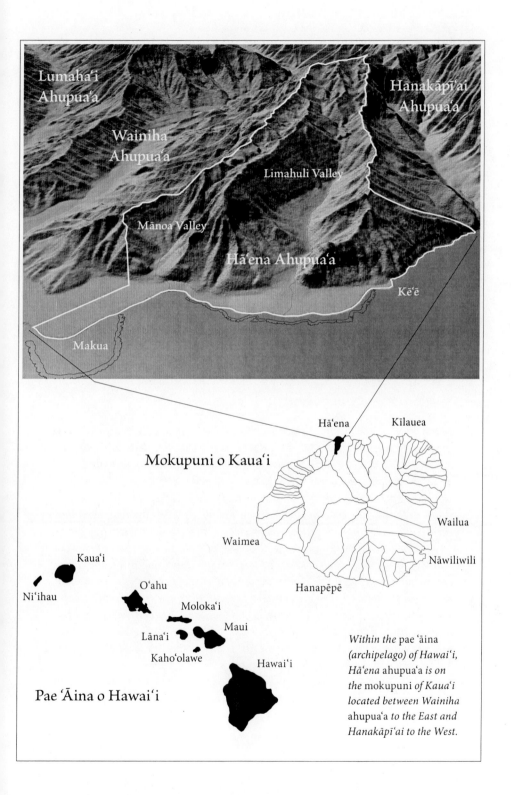

Within the *pae ʻāina (archipelago) of Hawaiʻi, Hāʻena* ahupuaʻa *is on the* mokupuni *of Kauaʻi located between Waniha* ahupuaʻa *to the East and Hanakāpīʻai to the West.*

to the taro patch. *Every day is taro patch. Then you go fishing. Because we catch our food first and then when we go down there, grandma is cooking her salt rice and then she* pūlehu *(broil over coals) the fish. And that's what we're going eat.* Wana *(sea urchin),* loli *(sea cucumber), raw* enenue *(chub fish), raw moonlight fish. Almost every fish I ate raw.* Hīnālea *(wrasse, family Labridae), raw,* pūlehu *or fry. All those things, but mostly* pūlehu *because* ʻono *(delicious), eh?*

Thomas: Like when I was growing up, young. Plenty (fish)! Like you go with the ʻoama *(young of the goatfish) net, one time you surround, one* pākini *(five-gallon galvanized tub)!* Pākini *by* pākini *they catch and* kaulaʻi *(dry in the sun). That's the only way you can preserve ʻum. And then you know you eat ʻum in different ways, like boiling, raw, fried.*

But that time, you see, the Hawaiians was more reserved, you know. They'd go catch only the big kind and only enough to eat. And that's how they used to fish before. Not the kind, you go for the kill. Nah. In fact, in my life we never did that. Because we were always cautious. You know, you have to leave some back. So you always get. And this place (Hāʻena) was always like that.

Women were important participants in the fishery. Mary Kahiliopualokelani Chu Wann was one of many elders who recalled the role of women as fishers in the *ahupuaʻa.*

Mary: The best heʻe *(octopus) place was right there in front of Koia (area in Hāʻena fronting the family lands). Yeah, she (Mary's mother) loved to do that (fishing for octopus). And she was good at it. You know from Limahuli stream to aunty Emma's place? From there, that (reef) flat. She had a skill that was her specialty. The* heʻe. *She had a long sharp spear and she had coconut. She had the coconut that was really, really oily. The kind that pulled away from the shell already, and she would chew it and chum the water with it and instead of using glass boxes.*

And then, she knows just how the heʻe *looks for a place to hide. They find a hole that they like and then they take all the sand out of the hole and rocks. They always excavate the hole, pull it up, so my mother can always look and she sees a mound. She knows there's a squid in there, so she goes with her spear and the next thing you know you see these tentacles come up and they come around the spear and they wrap themselves around the spear and she pulls them out hanging on to this spear.*

Right! And she gets the head and she just paralyzes them by just biting between the eyes. All of a sudden the tentacles, you can see the heʻe *let loose of her arm, of the spear and they're dead. I wouldn't try it. She liked to do that, never failed, always. So if we didn't have fish, we always had squid. That's the kind of life we lived.*

Violet: Yes, and if you like to go hook, upāpalu *(the larger cardinal fishes) is for night time, or* hīnālea *for daytime or that hard head fish. What do you call that hard head fish?* poʻopaʻa *(hawkfish—Cirrhites pinnulatus)? All the old people used to go hook that one. I still remember the* poʻopaʻa. *The old people love to make soup with that. But some of our people like the* hīnālea. *They used to dry 'um and then they used to* pūlehu *(broil over coals) that fish. That fish has a sweet, sweet smell.*

After the independence of the Hawaiian nation was taken away by the United States in 1898, the fisheries attached to each *ahupuaʻa* were ruled to be public domain and acquired by condemnation. The intent of the U.S. Congress was to open them up to all citizens of the new regime. Despite the fisheries being taken from the *ahupuaʻa* residents under this new system of laws, the belief that the community of each *ahupuaʻa* has the responsibility to care for its own reefs and fishing grounds still exists among the Native people, especially those of Hāʻena.

Certain rights were embedded in the deeds of the lands privatized during the early years of the Hawaiian nation. These rights included rights of access, fishing, water, and gathering. This meant that the great majority of government, crown, and *aliʻi* lands were subservient to the rights reserved for the people. This is still an integral part of the legal system that was set into place during the time when Hawaiʻi was an independent nation. However, when Euro-American forms of government began to displace traditional life ways, these rights, despite being a part of the legal code, came under attack by foreigners whose concepts of land use differed sharply from those of the aboriginal people. *Kūpuna* remember some of the things gathered from mountain, valley, and plain.

Nancy: Like ah, when tūtū *Wahinekeouli weaves her mats and hats. Have you seen a hat made out of maidenhair (fern) stem? Oh my* tūtū *made a hat, a beautiful hat using only the stems. My papa said it was from up the mountain, they use to go hunting, they would gather all the maidenhair stems for her, and that's what she used. And then she made hats out of that, and of course coconut,* lauhala *(pandanus), and* Kilipaki *(Gilbertese)* lauhala *leaves, which you had to boil and dry up.*

Thomas: We had to go ma uka *(inland). We went to get the banana, that you call the* maiʻa, *the one that grows straight up, the mountain banana, the orange one (the* feʻi *banana is a variety of Tahitian banana growing in Hāʻena). Because that* maiʻa, *the bark outside is all black. Like* maiʻa ʻeleʻele *(black). Yes, they used that for making designs. Then of course, they used the different colors of the* hala. *They have the light brown, and the white. You know, like weaving a name or whatever on the* moena *(mat). When it was gathering time you go get plenty. And then you strip everything out here, throw all the* ʻōpala *(rubbish) away, and take it (the*

*cleaned leaves) home and then you roll it roughly, roll it in big roll, just like wheels.
Like that, it's just to store it. And that's how we used to help. We go gather 'um and
do this. Just to make it easier for grandma or mama you know. We went through
the whole procedure doing all this stuff when we were young.*

The *kauhale,* or traditional grouping of houses, having the sleeping house separate from the cooking house and the other outbuildings, was one custom carried
over into post-American times. A few families in Hāʻena, longtime residents of
the area, still continue this separation of buildings by function.

*Mary Chu Wann, an heir
of Kamealoha, in 1958.
Presley Wann family
collection.*

*Mary: Ah, rough lumber. Those days they only used rough lumber. Okay, well
inside was smoothed out a little bit, but the house was redwood with rough lumber.
It was just one big room, a kitchen-dining room area where you had these long
benches and the table. Those days you had a cookhouse that was separated from
the main house. Because that cookhouse was not only used for cooking your meals,
but it was also used for cooking taro.*

Despite the tremendous impact other cultural perspectives and values had on
the evolution of law in Hawaiʻi and attempts of newcomers to expunge the provi-
sions placed in the law by Kauikeouli (Kamehameha III), the rights of Native

people to gathering, to water, to access mountains and sea, remain enshrined in contemporary statutes and the Hawai'i State Constitution.

WAHI PANA—THE STORIED LANDSCAPE

Place names reveal a great deal about any locality, and Hā'ena is no exception. Names given in older times still appear in records of ownership and other documents such as deeds and papers produced during the Westernization of Hawai'i. Government records are therefore a rich source of place names of any district. Testimony gathered during the changes from traditional land tenure to Euro-American concepts of private property found in the documents of the Mahele of 1848 and the Kuleana Act of 1850 provide one of the richest sources of important information about the people, the land, and its resources.

The following transcript of a dispute settled between the owners of two *ahupua'a* is a prime example of the wealth of information to be found about names of peaks and other features marking the boundaries of these two *ahupua'a*. This document identified the sea fronting Hā'ena as Hiala'a, while Koa'ekea was the name of the sea fronting neighboring Wainiha. Prior to uncovering this document, the names of the seas had been unknown to even the eldest of present-day residents of these two *ahupua'a*. It is very possible that in traditional times all of the seas fronting *ahupua'a* around the entire island and throughout the neighboring islands had names that have long been forgotten.

Kekauonohi (for L. Haalelea)*

This is a dispute for the border between Haena and Wainiha.

*Kanohi, sworn: (for Wainiha) I was born during the time of Kaumualii and raised in Wainiha, I have seen the boundaries of Haena and Wain-iha. The boundary mauka is Waialeale, running this way to **Kilohana;** from there to **Keaalewalewa** and to **Kapalikalahale,** to **Kaleleio** and to Peak **Kamanu.** The manu (bird?) were from Haena, the kanakas who did the work with the birds were from both Haena and Wainiha; from there the boundary runs to **Hanaimaa** and to **Hianakahee; Hialaa** is the sea over here and **Koaekea** is the sea of Wainiha. My parents had told me about these boundaries which I have given in the above statements.*

Kamaka, sworn: I have seen the boundary between Haena and Wainiha, Waialeale is the boundary mauka. I do not know where to go from there

---

**Author's note: The transcript was taken from *Native Testimony* vol. 10:398–399 - No. 10613 A. Paki, from page 239 Haena, August 23, 1854, protested by No. 11216 M. The names in bold are names of places in Hā'ena and Wainiha.*

*(Waialeale). Makai is **Lonoapii** and running to **Kaimamanu** on to **Puuiki**, then to **Keaalewalewa**. I do not know the boundaries to the land further mauka, but **Hianakahee** is the boundary by the beach which is a tier of stones. I had seen these boundaries when we came with "Kaili," an akua at the time of Kamehameha I to eat here in Kauai. We were the kahunas. I am now a kamaaina for Wainiha. I have sat in at "Huleia," in a settlement with Kahekili by their status as Konohiki only and I have known about the boundary since that time to the present.*

*Kiwaa, sworn: Waialeale is the boundary mauka of Wainiha and Haena's mountain, running from there to **Keaalewalewa** on the top of the ridge, then this way to Puuiki and to the puu ka, manu; from there to a place called "**Hinakahee**," a reef on the beach, I have seen, it is not hearsay.*

*Opu, sworn: (for Haena) I was born before the royal reign of Kaumualii here on Kauai when Kikala was the Konohiki, Luia, the tenant and Kamakolelani was the Konohiki of Wainiha. The boundary mauka is **Maunahina**, Haena runs this way along the ridge; when the rock rolls, it is for Wainiha, it is for Haena when it is lodged, then from Maunahina to **Peku** and on the Hanaimaa and finally running to the beach called "**Kapaenui**." These places make up the boundary between Wainiha and Haena. My parents Mauoli have been my informants for these boundaries. It was during the time of Kaumualii that I had actually seen the akua makahiki roll to "**Keahu**," so we took food and paid tribute. **Kapalikala- hale** is below and **Peku** is further above, then this way to **Leleio** on that side of Wainiha and this side of Haena, then on to **Hanaimaa** until **Kapaenui**. Meheula was the chief who had a double portion of food from these lands of Haena and Wainiha and I have heard my parents say that the boundary has moved until it has **Hinakahee** and there has been no objection to the border I've seen. Only now I see there is a dispute over these boundaries.*

*Kaukapawa, sworn: **Kaae** is the boundary makai, then it runs this way to **Hanaimaa**, then to **Kainamanu** and on until **Puuiki** to **Kapalikala- hale**. I had heard from my parents. I have lived there since the time of Kaeo and I am a true native for this land. **Hinakahee** is a celebrated place and the true boundary on the makai side is "**Kaeo**" or **Kapaenui**. I have heard from my parents that the boundary of Haena which is **Kanakahee** was given for Wainiha.*

MAKANA

An excursion through the *ahupua'a* of Hā'ena, walking from storied place to storied place, provides an opportunity to appreciate the richness of the connection of the people to the land and stories linking them to each other. Whether approaching Hā'ena from the sea or catching glimpses while driving toward it along the road, the peak Makana (Gift) dominates the landscape, giving this *ahupua'a* a unique look. When asked why such a name would be given to a mountain, a *kupuna,* disbelief expressed eloquently in his eyes, proceeded to explain as if to an unschooled child. Glancing out over the land and sea, he pointed out perennial streams and abundant springs, motioned toward the reefs, sandy beaches, wave-splashed lagoons, and protected bays, calling attention to the rich, dark soil carefully preserved behind numerous stone-walled terraces. Reflecting on his days spent in the mountain reaches and sheltered valleys, home to wild boar, mountain shrimp, orange trees, *'ōhi'a 'ai* (mountain apple) groves, wild coffee thickets, the fragrant haunt of *maile* and *mokihana* (vines and berries used for lei), "How could they help but name it Makana?" was his question.

Makana continues to link hula devotees to this place where the graduation ceremony of hula students completing rigorous training demanded of them took place from time immemorial well into historic times. Certain initiated men ascended the picturesque peak to await the coming of nightfall. After sundown, they would kindle a fire of special wood carried up expressly for the ceremony called *'ōahi* (firebrands). Firebrands ignited in the blaze were cast out over the seaward-facing cliff of the pyramid-like peak where an updraft produced by the prevailing wind buffeting the *pali* bore them up into the night sky. Witnesses recall the firebrands floating in the air far out over the coastal plain, showering sparks as they drifted down into the sea.

Differing accounts exist among old-timers as to when this ceremony was last officially performed. Some say it was during the pilgrimage of Queen Emma to visit the legendary island of Nihoa in the 1800s; others recall it differently. But they are unanimous about the importance this ceremony contributed to the identity of the place and the people who lived there.

Mary: You know the word Hailama (her grandfather's name), you know what that means, right? If you broke that into two words, hai *means to throw as you would a spear. You threw it aiming in the open or in the air or whatever.* Lama, *you know what lama means? The flame! See, in Hawaiian, what you do is how you get your name. People had a faster way of describing a person so that they gave you a name. You had a name, let's say your parents named you, but you were so good at one thing that when they want to say, "O Hailama" or someone, when you look at the Hawaiian word, they all had meaning and it relates to what you're doing. So he got that name, Hailama. And so now when I hear that name being used outside (of the family), "Hey, you know that is Hailama, that was his name."*

Hai means he's the one that threw this torch. The Hāʻena people, there's a certain time of the year that they have the hālau *(hula) up there. They have a big celebration—part of that celebration is throwing that torch. Hailama. There is one person that could climb. My grandmother says she worries because it was a very dangerous climb. And only a few people know how to climb that mountain. You had to have a path that you knew well. Any other way that you climbed, you would get into trouble. Evidently people had done it before and weren't successful. Hailama, he kept it a secret. In his later years he tried to relay that secret to a younger, guy, Uncle Laʻa.*

Kapeka: All I know is my father (Laʻa Mahuiki) said he was the last one (fire-thrower). Yeah, cause he said it was scary. He used to go with his father, that's how. That's how he'd go up there. And the ship came, eh, the king or queen, whatever, who was reigning that time, come on the big ship. Come down. And the ship stay outside. And then they wait for the throwing of that fire sticks. You know, it's nothing for fool around. Over there the wind is strong on top there. They crawl with all the sticks on their backs. That's how my father would go.

Violet Hashimoto Goto.
Photograph by Hauʻoli
Wichman, 2003.

Violet: My dad said the last fireworks was in 1928. That's the year that my brother Jack was born. That was the last time it happened. These people, he said, you watch them walk up the side of the mountain. Right up front. But you know why they could do that? Because during those days they had mana *(spiritual power). Their* mana *was strong. That's why, that kept them alive. That's why they could do what they did.*

Following are references made in *ʻōlelo noʻeau* (traditional proverbs) about Makana.

> *Lauaʻe o Makana.*
> *The lauaʻe fern of Makana.*
>
> *Famed in songs and chants is the lauaʻe that grows everywhere at Makana on Kauai. When crushed it has a scent similar to that of the maile and is often used with the pandanus fruit in making leis.*

Ka poli laua'e o Makana.
Makana, whose bosom is adorned with laua'e ferns.

Famed in songs and chants are the fragrant laua'e ferns of Makana, Kaua'i.
Pukui 1983: 166, Proverb Numbers 1949, 1542

Laua'e is still used today by lei makers as a spacer to hold *mokihana* (an endemic plant found nowhere else in the world except on Kaua'i and O'ahu) off the skin. The *mokihana* lei is much sought after despite the fact that the fragrant berries contain a strong oil that easily burns skin. Folded, pierced, and spaced between the berries, leaves of *laua'e* keep the *mokihana* off the skin. Folding crushes parts of the leaf, releasing a subtle fragrance that complements the scent of the *mokihana*. The *mokihana* lei is rarely seen today.

Nancy: *Laua'e o Makana. My brother use to go get the* laua'e, *Hawaiian* laua'e *and they use to go get* maile. *They would go in the back, you know, where the pond in the middle by the wet cave, on top the cave, someplace over there they use to go. And they go earlier and they get the* maile *for May Day and they get the* laua'e. *Oh, you can smell the* laua'e. *No more over there any more. I never did see any more* laua'e. *They're not real big, they short, they fat, but sweet smell. When you go in you smell only the aroma. You know smell only the aroma, and the Hawaiian* laua'e *strong, when on your neck like just like how you smell the* mokihana, *the* laua'e, *Hawaiian* laua'e *is just like that.*

> *Ka pali 'ōahi o Makana.*
> *The firebrand-hurling cliff of Makana.*

> *Palapala or hau wood was cut, thoroughly dried, and carried up the hillside to an imu (earth oven) and made ready to be lit. When dusk descended, the imu was lighted and the logs placed in it. When blowing of the wind was just right, the lighted log was hurled into the wind and borne seaward, high over the heads of the spectators, before dropping into the sea.*
> Pukui 1983: 165, Proverb Number 1532

> *Hea mai 'o Makana me he ipo ala,*
> *'ike i ke ahi lele, 'ike i ke ahi lele,*
> *ho'ohihi nā malihini.*

> *(Makana calls as if a sweetheart,*
> *see the leaping fire, see the flying fire,*
> *the strangers [visitors] are enraptured.)*
> "Nā U'i o Kaua'i," words by Claude Downey/Ida Malabey, music by John Noble

The hala *groves of Naue were celebrated in song and story. The* hala *flower is reputed to possess properties with which to make love potions. The leaf, or* lauhala, *was the raw material for mats, thatching and other necessities. Here, the shade of* hala *trees provide shelter from the sun on the then treeless, windswept coastal plain of Hāʻena, enjoyed by cowboy, fisherman's canoe, and others in the background. Photograph by Alfred Mitchell, 1892, Bishop Museum.*

NAUE

Nā hala o Naue ʻau i ke kai.
The hala trees of Naue swim out to sea.

The hala trees of Naue, Kauaʻi, seem to reach out to sea.
Pukui 1983: 242, Proverb Number 2212

Nā hala onaona a o Mapuana,
E Naue ʻoe i ka ʻoni a ke kai.

Fragrant hala grove of Mapuana,
you move with the surging of the sea.
"Nani Kauaʻi," composer Lizzie Alohikea

Naue, traditionally associated with Hāʻena, is no longer officially located in Hāʻena *ahupuaʻa* due to the boundary dispute mentioned earlier. It is now situated in the neighboring *ahupuaʻa* of Wainiha. Boundary disputes like the one between Abner Pākī, the original owner of Hāʻena, and the venerable Haʻaleleʻa, representing the *aliʻi* Kamāmalu, original awardee of Wainiha, were fairly commonplace in the years following privatization of land begun during the Mahele of 1848. The original deeds conveyed the lands in name alone with no accompanying metes and bounds. Naue, often mentioned in song and story, is located on a point on the northern end of the coastal plain shared by Wainiha and Hāʻena *ahupuaʻa*. Naue means to move or to tremble. Travelers on boats offshore, in good weather and bad, can attest to that jutting point seeming to move and tremble when viewed from the sea.

References in songs to the famous *hala* (pandanus) grove at Naue have both romantic and practical nuances. Literally, *mapuana* means soft, wafted fragrance (Pukui and Elbert 1986: 241). Mentioned in the sayings and songs, Mapuana was the younger sister of ʻAiwohikupua, who transformed himself into a *hala* tree that bore a special red fruit famed for its fragrance, instead of the more commonplace yellow found throughout the islands (Beckwith 1970: 533). The male flower (*hinano*) of the *hala* is known by Hawaiians to be an ingredient for love potions. Pictures of Hāʻena taken in the early 1900s show the coastal plain there barren of all but a few *hala* trees.

Kūpuna remember having an uninterrupted view from Kepuhi point to Mānoa—a distance of approximately two miles. Today, it is almost impossible to see more than a few hundred yards, as the plain is entirely covered with a forest of alien trees and shrubs introduced from foreign places and a plethora of houses.

Hala leaves (*lauhala*) were used for weaving mats and hats and for house thatching. Weavers favored leaves from trees growing near the sea, as they were tougher and more durable, possibly due to constant weathering by the salt-laden wind sweeping in off the sea. Though the *hala* grove at Naue was imbued with emotional and mythical properties, it also was a practical resource, providing shade for the work of harvesting and preparing the durable leaves for making mats and other useful items.

"Naue i ka ʻoni a ke kai."
*Photograph by Hauʻoli
Wichman, 2007.*

Thomas: Nā hala o Naue. You know we used to come here (Naue) go pick hala. *Cut all the heads off from the* hala *leaves and take the* ʻōpala *(rubbish) off down here and we'd take home only the* hala, *the* kūkū *(thorns) all* hemo *(removed). When I go with mama, go get* hala, *it's the whole day. My mom was weaving and then of course grandma. Ihilani. Grandma Martha Kane. That's my mom's mom. She was a weaver.*

Most of the time they used to make moena *(mats) for the house. Oh yes, they'd make it according to the size of the room. The* maka *(weft) used to be wide. I think, one and a half inch. And then the only one made narrow one is for dinner napkins. And that's the only one they'd make small, half-inch. And then to just like engrave or I don't know how you going to say it, is they used to use the banana fibers. For design right?*

Violet: Oh yeah. I used to go pick lauhala *with my* tūtū. *Actually it's just above where Naomi folks' house, Naomi folks' property is located, outside of Camp Naue. That's where had all that* lauhala. *Because you know* tūtū *Ihilani, she used to weave hats and mats, and things like that. We used to go help her go pick up* lauhala.

During the war they used that place for... that's where the marines and the army had their donkey path like. Because it was all lauhala *and they could hide 'em all underneath there. Yeah, had one big camp at Naue. The tidal wave of '46 destroyed all the* lauhala, *all five acres (and all the way to the* kahakai, *all the way to the beach). That's what happened.*

MAKUA

Let us go and drink the water of Wailua, bathe in the water of Namolokama, eat the mullet that swim in Ka Wai Makua at Hāʻena, wreath ourselves with the moss (sea lettuce) of Polihale, then return to Oʻahu and dwell there.
Kamakau 1961: 187

The above statement is attributed to Kamehameha I, who was trying to inspire his warriors to invade Kauaʻi, the only island he had not conquered. As it turned out, Kauaʻi was the only island he did not successfully invade. Kaumualiʻi, *mōʻī* (paramount leader) of Kauaʻi, presented Kamehameha with an agreeable diplomatic solution, alleviating the necessity for an invasion of conquest. In this saying of Kamehameha, who had presumably never been to Kauaʻi, he lists names identifying *wahi pana* of Kauaʻi, illustrating the considerable significance these places had even to people of other islands. The bay at Makua provides a safe landing for canoes for most of the year. The reefs there were, and continue to be, a primary source of food for the Native Hawaiian community.

The reference to eating mullet swimming in "the waters of Makua" (Ka-Wai-Makua) illustrates the importance of this place even to outlanders who made up the army of the Hawaiʻi island *aliʻi*. Fresh water flowing into the bay at Makua (Mānoa stream) and the *pōhaku ʻalā* (water-worn basalt stone) deposited nearby the stream mouth attract the *ʻanae* (large oceangoing mullet), fish frequenting areas where fresh water flows into ocean. Basaltic rock provides the right medium for algae, a favorite food of mullet, to grow. The *ʻanae* follow a pattern of travel that brings them regularly into the area to feed on the algae when tide and time are right. Contemporary fishermen still seek the mullet in this area referred to by Kamehameha I so many years ago.

Makua has long been a favored place for fishermen of the *ahupuaʻa* of Hāʻena. More recently, even visitors participate in the yearly harvest of schooling *akule* (*Trachurops crumenophthalmus*—big-eyed scad). This event was traditionally a community effort to net large numbers of the fish during the summer, when they aggregated in the calm waters of the sheltered bay. Fish caught were distributed to all participants, to visitors or anyone who lent a hand, and in some instances, even to those who were only observers.

Papaloa (long reef) (Wichman 1998: 124), the reef sheltering Makua, begins almost at the sand beach rounding the tip of the headland there. It curves seaward and back to the land, forming the closest thing to a lagoon found on the island. This rich resource provides a constant source of food for the people of Hāʻena, which is perhaps another reason for the name, meaning parent. The lagoon and reef also provided shelter to ocean travelers seeking protection and respite from the rough seas common to this coast.

Papaloa, the long reef of Makua, "ice box, medicine chest, and retirement plan" for generations. Limahuli Garden collection, 2002

Like other bays on the island, this one, clinging to the western shoulder of Makua reef and fronting the beach at Maniniholo, is a favored place to surround the schools of several species of fish aggregating there at different times of the year. Catching fish, always a community activity, requires specialized nets and teams of men to man the boats setting and retrieving them. People are also needed to patch, dry, store, and keep the nets ready for use during fishing season. Older folks and children, both male and female, usually do the maintenance work on the nets, for they cannot do the arduous work of rowing the boats, diving down—sometimes in twenty or thirty feet of water—to move the nets once they are set, or hauling the nets toward the shore after the fish have been surrounded.

Nancy: Oh, he (John Hanohano Pā) had some men work for him go patch net. My brothers, we all had to learn to help my papa to patch the net all inside Makua. When we stay down there we have to help him gather the net for dry and then gather and tie 'um up and put 'um away for the next time. My brothers was all old enough to patch and then what we do is they lay the net on top the stick to spread 'um out for dry. We all help them.

An important person in this community endeavor, the *kilo iʻa* (fish spotter), kept a constant eye on the ocean during the season. Since most of the men in the community were fishermen, they also kept watch on the sea while they worked or were engaged in other activities. The *kilo iʻa,* however, was a specialized seer. Observing the color and movement of the fish, he could discern the species, the age, and approximately how many pounds (or how many baskets, the measurement used in the past) of fish were contained in the school. From a high point on the land, using a system of hand signals, flags, shouts, and sometimes whistles, the *kilo iʻa* directed the boats setting out the nets. In Hāʻena, the proximity of the cliffs to the ocean provided a perfect vantage point for *kilo iʻa.*

Laʻa Mahuiki was a well known *kilo iʻa* during his lifetime. He was able to confirm to the men whether the school present in the bay was worth catching. For instance, if a school of big *ʻōʻio* (*Albula vulpes*—bonefish) was in the bay, he would warn the men off. Although a good food source, this fish was not desirable because the many small bones in its flesh made it hard to sell in modern times. It was also important that the nets used for *ʻōʻio* were strong enough. *ʻŌʻio* are a strong fish, sometimes the size of small sharks—some say as long as a man's leg—so they are capable of making holes in nets. When this happened, all the fish escaped, making for a lot of wasted time and effort. In addition, the community then had to spend many hours patching the holes, so the nets would be ready when the next school arrived.

Violet: *Oh, that was so much fun because* tūtū *Laʻa and* tūtū *Hanohano, they were fishermen. They had their fishing huts down on the beach where you cook, you eat, everything.* Tūtū *Laʻa, he used to be on the hill. From our place we can see him. We hear the whistle blow, we see the flag going, we all go down there. But now no can see because of all the trees. He used to sit on that mountain, we'd see his flag go up, blow his whistle, then everybody go down there and everybody go help pull the net down at Maninihola.*

They used to even fish right inside Makua. The akule *all come right inside there. And* tūtū *Hanohano had his sampan. And used to get plenty boats, you know the Rices, and all the people that used to live over here. All their boats were inside here and we used to swim all in there. Had plenty fish during that time. Like the* ʻoama. *Get so much* ʻoama. *You catch what you like and that's it. So much.*

In later years not all fishermen climbed the cliff to view the fish.

Thomas: *Whoever was the fisherman they'd go* kilo *their own. But like us guys, we* kilo *right from the beach. We no go climb on top there because no need go, we can see the fish. In other words, we would* kilo *from over here, Hale Pōhaku. You know, you can look ʻum already. You no need look ʻum in the deep because you no more* *net for go way outside there in the deep. So what? You going wait until they come inside, because your net is limited you know. And that's the way it was.*

The owner of the nets and boats was a very important figure in the community, as sometimes more than a single boat was necessary to lay the nets out. John Hanohano Pā was one such man. Stories told by different people of the *ahupuaʻa* illustrated that Hanohano Pā epitomized traditional values of an *ahupuaʻa* leader. A fisherman of note in a community of fishermen, his strength as a swimmer was legendary.

The diving equipment used by *kūpuna* to manage the nets set in the deep water of the bay during these early years was very primitive compared to what is available today.

Thomas: No more the kind aqualung stuff in those days, and the caves are deep, you know! Skin diving. When we used to fish with them, they only had those goggles made from hau *(a soft-wooded hibiscus) with glass. And that's all they had, not this kind goggles we get now days.*

It was the kind socket on the eye. It's either that or the Japanese one, you know, those turtle shell, they had, eh? The only problem with that was it was going dig your eye. He going sink inside your eye if you go deep. Not like the hau. *The* hau *was kind of gentle on the eye. You know, it would suck your eyes but not the kind way to hurt. And then after you* pau *dive, get all scar right around your eye.*

That hau *kind. You got to make your own, glue the glass on it and waterproof that thing so that the water no go inside. The water go inside, you know, going come blur. You no can see nothing. Oh yes, they dive bare eye. But you know that's strenuous for the eye.*

Community members said Hanohano Pā had good luck catching fish because he always gave part of his catch to the people. Only after he had given enough fish away to satisfy the needs of the community (much of the fish was dried for future use) would he send fish to the markets on the other side of the island, where fish peddlers would in turn sell them to the plantation labor communities. It was said that because he gave away fish, more schools of fish would come into the bay, providing him and the community with plenty. His generosity, and the ability to provide food for the community, reflected characteristics of an ideal *aliʻi* of more ancient times, but he would not necessarily have articulated it in that way. During his most active years, Hanohano Pā owned a large sampan that he kept anchored in Makua during the calmer times of the year (usually summers). Thomas Hashimoto, still actively fishing in his seventies, recalled that when the high surf season began in the fall, the large vessel would be hauled up the sand dunes (about ten to twelve feet high) on the point in the lee of the reef at

*John Hanohano Pā on vacation
in the continental U.S.
Lono Brede family collection.*

Makua, the parent, the place,
feeding and sheltering Hāʻena
hoaʻāina *for millenia.*
Photograph by Alfred Mitchell,
1892, Bishop Museum.

Makua. Laying a series of planks on the sand, community members put wooden rollers under the hulls, then used pulleys, animals, and vehicles when available to haul the boat out to sit high and dry during the rough winter months.

Kupuna Samson Mahuiki spoke of the small reefs bordering the shore in the deep recesses of the bay at Makua on the shore side of the deep channel leading into the leeward end of the lagoon there. Those little reefs, only a short walk away from his home, provided food for his family for as long as he could remember. Though they offered a convenient source of fresh fish, he stressed that they never abused the area, only using it sparingly, reserving it for times when the outer

Samson in his youth with his mother Rachel.
Samson Mahuiki family collection.

reefs were awash and dangerous in the winter. His mother, Rachel, was recognized as the best catcher of *he'e* (octopus) in her time, bar none, man or woman. A master of those skills women practiced in traditional *ahupua'a* life, she was closely watched by others interested in learning the secrets of successfully catching *he'e*. Some of these would often notice her walking to the beach and try to get to the *he'e* grounds before her if they saw any hint that she might be heading that way.

Samson: Oh, the heʻe, *that's a skill that plenty guys would like to beat her at. But if you cannot see good, and if the squid never move and if you had spooked them and you cannot see 'um, you not goin' pick them up. But because you had spook 'um, any movement he made going show the indention. So one trained eye, picks all that up. So that's the trouble when one guy who doesn't know how to tell those signs, (he is) jammed up. He sets it up for the (real) squid man.*

When she (Rachel) goes down there, she no take nothing spear the way every-body does because somebody else (might) see and think, eh, must be a good time (for catching heʻe) *because they saw her going. I mean, the good guys, they not going fishing unless it is guarantee! So that's why you gotta know how to read sign, eh...So she never did take anything when she go down the beach, so nobody would know where she was going.*

Nancy: I did learn from Aunty Rachel and of course I wear my eyeglasses. She tell me for bite the eye. You know by the time I bite the eye the black water (octopus ink) shooting on me and the leg all turning. You have to peel 'um, or else you have to turn the head inside out then all right. Oh the leg, the first time the legs went inside my eyeglasses, all tangle up.

Rachel was also adept at fishing the inner reefs in ways not practiced today. Often she would catch reef fish with her bare hands, reaching into holes near the beach where the fish would take refuge when the outer sea was rough. She knew not to reach into the holes when eels were present, an ever present danger when doing this type of fishing. Grandma Rachel, a noted singer, a source of wisdom and knowledge about traditional customs, was an inspiration to younger genera-tions of Hawaiians active in community initiatives. Samson also recalled how his mother showed her children a unique method of gathering fish from nearby Limahuli stream, using a method probably never seen today.

Samson: Just wall 'em (one branch of Limahuli stream) with the stones and mud, so simple. The thing was so easy, we even catch ʻoʻopu *(a freshwater goby), any small opening on the side that's where the* ʻoʻopu *going be. So in those ditches, whooo, loaded. All the side streams were loaded.*

Well, that's what we use to do, eh? And the other thing we use to do when we like ʻoʻopu *if, if my mother like* ʻoʻopu, *we, we block the stream, Yeah, down Koia, get the one (branch of the stream) that goes down by Taylor Camp. Take taro patch mud and wall 'em with the stone and mud. Seal 'em with the mud.*

Sometimes, we use, you know, an old trunk. Used to bust the bottom out, put chicken wire, and then go look where there was a good drop (in an irrigation ditch) and put 'em right in. Make sure the bottom is in the water. The ʻoʻopu *fall in! We used to pick up four o'clock in the afternoon. If they drop in, they stay in the trunk.*

The only thing going get jammed up if somebody going go up there before us and be jealous that we catching all this 'o'opu.

But I look at her, you know, everything take time. But, she was the one show us how to block the stream. No need special equipment, just take that mud and seal that water. She was very knowledgeable for the reef as well. Oh what you call, food supply from the reef, like with the loli, *with the* wana, *the* pukas, *how to use 'em.*

MANINIHOLO

Moving westward along the bay at Makua, the next storied place is Maniniholo, sometimes pronounced or spelled Maninihola (*manini*, convict tang, and *holo*, to travel or to run). Maniniholo, the beach area and cave associated with the tradition of Pele digging in search of a home, embraces the general area fronting the cave, including the beach and shallows lying in front of Hā'ena Beach Park. In another story explaining the origin of the cave Maniniholo, a Menehune protecting his catch of fish from mischievous *e'epa* (mysterious beings with extraordinary powers), dug out the cliff face, trying to get those imps out of the crevices and fissures in the lava rock where they were hiding (Wichman 1998: 127).

The diminutive *manini*, favored by the old folks, love special green *limu* (seaweed) sprouting and growing on rocks and reefs of Hā'ena, especially in the winter when freshly scoured by rough seas. Older Hawaiians often eat *manini* (*Acanthurus triostegus*—convict tang), a favorite reef fish celebrated in song and at mealtime. They consume the whole fish, including the stomach, which contains a special *limu* considered a delicacy by the people of old. After eating all the stomach and flesh, some even chew and crush the bones as I saw eighty-something John Hanohano Pā do one day, his still strong, excellent teeth effortlessly reducing the bones to pulp, sucking out all of the juices and leaving only a small pile of crushed bone fragments on his plate.

Thomas: *Plenty* i'a *(fish). He come automatic like that. Like before you come over here and the* wai *(water) little bit more high than this? All over here,* manini. *All* manini *come eat the* pahapaha *or the* 'ele'ele *(two varieties of seaweed).*

Pōhaku alā, embedded in the sandstone and coral outcroppings clinging to the sandy shore area in front of the cave, are uncovered by large winter waves and scoured with drifting sand. *Kūpuna* relate that when the surf is very large, the *manini* desert their holes farther out on the reef in deeper water because the water becomes too turbulent for them to stay there. The schools travel into sheltered water inside the reef nearer to the beach, becoming more accessible to the people.

Older fishermen share practical insights they learned both from their elders and from their own fishing experiences. They stress that this knowledge came through the application of common sense and keen, systematic observation.

All the fishermen spoke of the elders' intense study of the *limu* growing on the reefs for indications that grazing fish swimming up onto the reefs during the high tides were frequenting the area.

Good fishermen knew the traveling patterns of the schools, so when the fish were scared from one site and ran to alternate sites, fishermen would anticipate their movements and be there waiting. They knew during which season the different types of fish were fat and when they were skinny. They also understood conservation. They often repeated the sentiment "just catch enough to eat," acknowledging that all families depended on the reefs for fish and all who fished had a responsibility to ensure a continuing supply.

Things have changed as people from other cultures have come to far outnumber Native Hawaiians in Hāʻena. Many of these newcomers have no knowledge of the traditional fishing system that provided for families in the past. The reefs of an *ahupuaʻa* were considered part of the cultivated areas utilized for food. *Ahupuaʻa* residents left reef areas alone so fish could graze undisturbed, only accessing the reefs when food gathering was necessary. Newcomers often fish at all times without regard to the rhythms of the moon and tides, scaring the fish and keeping them skittish and "skinny." Most continental people are not aware of indigenous practices or the needs of the resident Native community. From the perspective of the Native people, these newcomers tromp through their ancestral gardens taking inappropriately, for sport, recreation, and trophy bragging rights, and should be more sensitive to traditional and customary practices. Prior to the coming of Europeans, an estimated 800,000 to a million people (Stannard 1989) survived in these islands, without any food coming in from other lands. Fish was a primary source of protein. How did they manage to do it?

Violet: Tūtū *Hanohano,* tūtū *Laʻa Mahuiki, Tom Mahiula Hashimoto, Jacob, Simeon Maka, all were net fishermen. They lived in Hāʻena. Throwing net in those days, had plenty fish, Hāʻena, the beach had plenty fish. Not anymore. It's really changed, times have changed.*

Thomas: We get! We get kole *(an especially esteemed, delicious surgeonfish). But you know we used to go spearing before when we were young. You know when we were in our teens. We make wire spears with the fence wire. We use the kind bamboo for the sling and go make the tube rubber for shoot fish. We used to catch.*

And sometimes you know we used to go look for the akule or manini pile. And they go under the ʻāpapa (reef). So you look under the ʻāpapa, you fire under there you catch four, five with one shot. That's what used to happen before.

Only enough for eat. And that's how they used to fish before. Not the kind you go for the kill. Nah. In fact, in my life we never did do that. Haʻawi (give) aloha

and eat, that's what it was. And it wasn't the kill. We'd catch enough, pau. *Because
we always cautious. And thinking about you know, you leave some back. So you
get. So you always get. And this place was always like that. Like now, with less guys
fishing, only Moku folks fish besides me, you no see fishermen outside the* 'āpapa.
You know, only us. But less fish. Why? I don't know.

MĀNOA

> *Manoa. Numerous, very many*
> *Mānoa. Thick, solid, vast*
> Pukui and Elbert 1986: 239

Leaving the shoreline and following the stream inland that in dry seasons loses
itself in the sand of the beach at Maniniholo, the valley of Mānoa slopes upward.
It once contained an extensive complex of *lo'i* (irrigated terraces for growing
taro). Past a spidery waterfall, the stream hides itself away in a hanging valley.
An extraordinary little valley, like Limahuli, the other main valley of Hā'ena,
Mānoa is cut by perennial streams. It is the site of an extensive cluster of stone-
faced terraces interwoven with an intricate network of *'auwai* (waterways). In
times past the valley supported an abundance of taro, providing the staple vegetable food complementing the fish gotten from the sea. A walk up the small
stream from the dip in the road just before Maniniholo cave leads to many stone
walls defining the complex *lo'i* climbing stair-like up the valley sides into the
cool green interior. These *lo'i* must have presented an impressive sight in traditional and early historic times when the land was clear and cultivating taro was
essential to the survival of the people.

Today, trees and shrubs cover once productive fields, filling the valley with
shadows. *'Auwai* no longer carry water to the waiting taro. The aquifer, tapped
by a government well, now supplies water to the growing number of residential
and vacation rental homes built on the nearby coastal plain fronting the valley
stretching toward Wainiha, leaving the once productive *lo'i* only a memory of a
different time. In other parts of Hā'ena, however, *lo'i* are being restored and *kalo*
cultivation is increasing.

Mike Olanolan, who has lived in proximity to Mānoa most of his life, spent
his formative years hunting and fishing with the older generation in the high-
lands above Mānoa. He spoke of a time when Mānoa provided passage into the
higher mountains for expeditions to gather forest products and to hunt feral pigs
or search for wayward cattle. In traditional times, bird catchers from Hā'ena
traveled to the uplands to harvest the *ua'u* (shearwater), spoken of in the chronicles of the Menehune and in testimony regarding the boundaries of Hā'ena. In

Mānoa, gateway to the mountain lands.
Photograph by Hauʻoli Wichman, 2007.

earlier times, these sea birds were a source of food—considered a delicacy when taken while fat prior to fledging and preserved in oil-filled calabashes. Today, the *uaʻu* is an endangered species, due to feral rats, cats, and dogs attacking these ground-burrowing sea birds nesting in the uplands. Before 1960, free-roaming cattle and horses grazed high on the ridges and higher reaches of the valleys, keeping trails open and making it much easier for people to get into the uplands. In traditional and early historic times, families depended entirely on the products of the land and sea for survival, and there was much more traffic to and from the uplands. Today, vines, brush, and trees, many of which are invasive alien species, cover most of this area, making access more difficult.

The rising lands of Mānoa provided a refuge for certain families on April 1, 1946, when a destructive tsunami swept over the sandy stretches of Naue, pouring across the coastal plain and heading west toward Makua behind the higher sand dunes of the coast. Bulldozing through homes, the school, and church where families had taken refuge, it claimed lives—scarring the memories of the people and changing the face of the land. Those who succeeded in reaching the higher lands of Mānoa before the ocean scoured the land survived to tell the story.

Samson: In '46 no we never had this house. This house was built in '73, '74. The old house was there, though. The old house would have been a hundred years. The old house, now it's gone. That's what they call Hale Makua.

That morning was April 1st. When we went to school, my two brothers George and Tom. And the first thing I could think of was for my dog. My dog and my cat. 'Cause they were my buddies, my cat and my dog. And my dog he was running around and Hā'ena was washed out. Our house, that was the house in the back, there was pushed off its foundation. Anyway was all damaged. We stayed at grandma's. (Juliette Wichman's home located on higher ground became a shelter for the displaced families in the wake of the catastrophe.)

My mom got caught in the tidal wave. And at that time when they were here, Mom had tūtū Hanohano. He had his wife, Julia. He was married to Julia Crowell. She had a daughter, Nona. They were living right next door, so she was always with my mom. And my mom was hāpai (pregnant) with Junior that time. It happened in April and Junior was born in July. Old man Hanohano said, "There's a tidal wave." Because these two ladies went go down the beach to look. How you like that? Get one tidal wave!

Old man Hanohano told them to get home! So they came home. They only had reach by the house. They never know nothing what had happened. The tidal wave hit. The big wave. They got swept off their feet.

There were all those java plum trees in the back here. They got caught in the plum tree. That's how they saved themselves. Hanging on to the plum branch. But they got caught. And then my mom them never had any clothes on because the current was so strong. So she and tūtū Hanohano's wife, they came on this high ridge over here and they had to walk all the way. They climbed up on the mountain in the back there. But still they had to swim in the back there. Because get one just like drain here and this is the main stream for draining all of back here? So they walked on the ridge over here and then up on the mountain to go to Wainiha.

There was a Mormon church just where Lahela folks live. There was a Mormon church over there. So they all came to the church thinking that they going come in the Mormon church, they would be saved. That's where twelve people got killed.

In 1957, another tsunami swept through Hā'ena, doing much damage to property but not taking life. This time people did not mistake it for an April Fool's prank.

Kapeka: 1957 I witnessed. Well, you hear just like a rifle shot and that's the waves coming in. The wave was coming more high, more high. They had go down from that hill and run back. Run back to Paweaka (a reef area nearby) by the turn. And the wave passed them. Huh, I was so mad. They'd run for their life.

That tidal wave was in March, March 9th, 1957. My dad he was sitting on the porch and before when never had these trees, from our old house you could see the

ʻāpapa *down there, you could see the ocean. He was sitting on the porch and patching his net. But on the radio, Lucky Luck (a popular disc jockey of the time) kept repeating and repeating that exactly at 8 o'clock going get one tidal wave. So my dad said, "Well, you kids, you folks better get up and get ready and pack food and pack the pots and pack this." (The entire family) went down to Grandma Wichman's.*

No more trees, can see the ocean. The kai (sea) that morning was nice. The ʻāpapa was dry, was dry and malia *(calm), you know the sea. So we packed up and while going down we told our neighbors like the Maka and the Mahuiki families, "Oh you know, get one tidal wave warning." They never listen to us, but we had our food packed, everything, blankets.*

So we moved out, we stayed over there. We went straight over there. We had the radio. Then when came 8 o'clock, eh, he was right. Because we were looking at the ocean all of a sudden the ocean came real dry. It pulled all the way back. This is it.

But me being so nosey I went on Uncle Hobie's. You know Uncle Hobie; get one big rock on his place. You can look all over, yeah. I went over there and sat on that rock. Everybody was gone. But I sat on that rock and I watched everything. You know outside here, this ʻāpapa over here, get that channel between the outside ʻāpapa and the inside ʻāpapa. No more nothing water. Dry. Down Maninihola, dry. All the water got pulled out way behind, pulled all the way outside. You know how you see the bugga building up, but inside all dry. Seeing is believing.

Violet: *It's beautiful (the bottom, the floor of the ocean). I seen it, I seen what this ʻāpapa had look like and the ʻāpapa outside. Beautiful in the formations, you know all the little ʻāpapa underneath. Then get that channel over there. No more nothing. You only see down to the sand. All the way, even down Maniniholo. You would think you could see some fish splattering, splattering around. But I guess when the waves pull out the fish go with it. Beautiful, you know how it looks on the ocean bottom. Beautiful formations, beautiful!*

Then when it starts coming in, when the first wave comes in it just fills in "whoosh." Like that, it just goes smooth. It just moves. And all what you could see was the tops of the trees. That's all. When it moves in it moves like that. Yes, that's Mother Nature. Right?

Well the first three (waves) is about the biggest. Yeah, it comes in and then it pulls back, everything. Then you going see all the rubbish. Everything, all going outside. The three first ones are about the biggest. And after that then it calms down. But then the whole day, it's going to be like that. Not big ones though. The action's going to be like that.

Mr. Maka, he was still living that time. He was a hard head. The Mahuiki and some of his Maka family, when we left, we told them to get out. You know what they did? They went go down the beach to go look if was for sure was going

*get one tidal wave. They had no time. They had to get out so fast, they just had
pass by Grandma's place right by the road, the first wave had hit. Otherwise, Mr.
Maka he was trying to run away, he got caught, his truck was smashed against
the tree. But he was okay. He said as soon as that had happen he went get out
of the truck and he had run for the hills.*

*Oh Mrs. Maka was so mad with him, Myra. She was so mad with him. 'Cause
she was hiding up there. When they could come back, she found him, he was inside
his house, he was eating. How mad she was with him. Then he was telling his story,
how the tidal wave had get him and he had run away, he had run up in the hills.
But the car was all smashed, you would think he died.*

*Yes, all the houses were pushed off their foundations. Even our old house was
pushed off its foundation, that's all. The county had big kind machines. Everybody
help each other clean up.*

Tsunami must have been a part of life in traditional times, but today's warning
systems were not developed until after the 1946 wave. Who knows how many of
these catastrophic waves have swept through Hā'ena since its first settlement or
how these waves affected the living patterns there before the written record was
available?

To the west of Mānoa, Limahuli sits higher in elevation than its sister valley.
The coastal plain there was not as thickly settled, and so records of tsunami
damage there are almost nonexistent. Many families surviving the tsunami
that scoured the plains fronting Mānoa had family-cultivated plots on the rising
alluvial ground fanning out from the mouth of Limahuli. After the waves of 1946
and 1957, many families, disheartened by their losses, left Hā'ena permanently.
Those remaining stayed alert for any sign of tsunami. Modern technology—
civil defense sirens, coordinated Pacific tsunami stations, and more efficient
television coverage—now allows for better advance warnings.

In the initial years following the tsunami, people were hesitant about living
in Hā'ena. Since the 1960s, however, many newcomers arriving from the U.S.
continent, having no idea how destructive the tsunami were in the past in that
area, eagerly bought up the available land. More houses are built each year.
Hā'ena is probably more densely populated now than it was in pre-European
times. Luckily, there has not been a serious tidal wave since 1959. The recent
tsunami in southeastern Asia have certainly provided graphic evidence of the
destructive power of the ocean to support testimony of *kūpuna* who survived
the waves in Hā'ena.

KĒʻĒ

> *Kilioe wahine i uka.*
> *Kilioe, woman of the upland.*

> *Kilioe was a wahine moʻo (lizard woman) famed in chants and songs of the aliʻi. She belonged to Kauaʻi and it was she who tried to prevent Hiʻiaka from taking the body of Lohiʻau from a cave at Hāʻena.*
> Pukui 1983: 193, Proverb Number 1799

> *I ka pau ana o keia mele a Pele i ka hea, ua nalowale honua iho la o "Kilioe' ma 'ikapua;" a komohia iho la iloko o na mea a pau ka hoohuoi wale ana, 'he mau wahine moo io no ka paha keia mau wahine malihini i hiki mai ai."*
> *Ke hoomaopopo pu la no hoi lakou i na olelo a ka wahine ipo a Lohiau i hoike mua mai ai no Kilioeikapua a me Kalanamainuu: oiai, ua lohe wale no lakou, he mau wahine kiai no ia no ka pali o Ke-e i Haena.*
> Hooulumahiehie 1906: Buke II, Helu 20, Pōʻakahi, Iune 25

> *(When Pele finished her chanting, Kiliʻoe and her fellow* moʻo *disappeared. Everyone there commented excitedly, "These were truly* moʻo *women indeed, these strangers that came here!" They all remembered the story that the sweetheart of Lohiʻau revealed about Kiliʻoeikapua and Kalanamainuʻu. They had only heard that they were the guardian women, indeed, for the cliffs of Kēʻē.)*

Kēʻē is where the coastal plain comes to an end against the ramparts of Nā Pali. The corrugated cliffs begin here, and the fringing reefs of Haleleʻa disappear along a coast where the deep ocean batters the basalt base of the mountains rising up in the center of the island. Kēʻē is where Pele enjoyed her interlude with Lohiʻau, and where Hiʻiaka battled the *moʻo* women in the cliffs and successfully revived the lover of her sister after his first unfortunate death.

Located at the end of the paved road, a trail leading from Kēʻē provides access to the cliffs standing over what is probably the most famous site associated with the hula in all of Hawaiʻi. Although *hālau hula* (institutions for learning hula) existed in other places in Hawaiʻi, Kēʻē and its related sites have the most extensive recorded history. The primary story associated with this place is that of Pele, Lohiʻau, and Hiʻiaka. In fact, the site of Lohiʻau's house is a recorded archaeological feature (Emory 1929: 94). The name Kēʻē literally means avoidance. In sayings, Kēʻē means great distances and trouble. *Aia i Kēʻē* (there at Kēʻē) is an old proverb referring to something that is too far away to bother about (Pukui, Elbert, and Moʻokini 1974: 105).

References to Kili'oe and Kalanamainu'u, two *mo'o* (beings of lizard- or dragon-like aspects) women who confronted Pele when she arrived at Hā'ena, speak of a Hawaiian belief about ancestors of the distant past who take on the form of animals in order to associate with the world of living human beings. In the story of Pele, Lohi'au, and Hi'iaka, the *mo'o* women suspect Pele is no ordinary mortal and challenge her, trying to get her to reveal her true identity. Pele makes short work of them in a battle of wits and words, revealing their identities as *mo'o* guardians of the cliffs of Kē'ē and sending them into hiding.

Later in the story, these *mo'o* women steal Lohi'au's spirit out of his body after he dies in the wake of his love affair with Pele and hide it in a cave high in the

Windswept Kē'ē. Pu'e one (sand dunes) line the Hā'ena coastline and are the traditional burial sites of the Native people. Bishop Museum.

cliffs above Kē'ē. Sent by Pele to retrieve her sister's lover, Hi'iaka spies the lingering spirit of Lohi'au near the entrance of the cave, beckoning wistfully to her. Hi'iaka and her traveling companion Wahine'ōma'o climb to the cave despite serious assaults by the *mo'o* women, eventually defeating them after an exhaustive battle. It is at Kē'ē that Hi'iaka and Wahine'ōma'o restore the spirit of Lohi'au to his body and nurse him back to good health (Emerson 1978).

Kili'oe, the *mo'o* woman, remains in Hā'ena today in the form of a stone, readily identifiable by its curiously honeycombed surface and its huge size. It is located at the base of the cliffs northwest of the *heiau* Keahualaka, just before

Ka Ulu o Paoa, the inspiration of Paoa, hula master and companion of Lohiʻau.
Photograph by Piliāmoʻo © 2007.

the cliffs of Nā Pali begin. At one time it was a *pōhaku piko* (umbilical cord stone), a place where people would hide the dried remnants of umbilical cords from their babies that fell off some days after birth. One purpose of this ritual was to connect the child spiritually with the land of his or her birth. Kenneth Emory, a noted twentieth-century archaeologist, considered the custom as "the material link with the past, along which was communicated the spiritual power of ancestors" (quoted in Barrère, Pukui, and Kelly 1980: 103, 146).

The *heiau* complex at Kē'ē contains several sites of note. Keahualaka (the altar of Laka) commemorates Laka, the patron deity of the hula. Kauluapaoa (the inspiration of Paoa) is also an important site located in the area. Paoa, an *ali'i* and close companion of Lohi'au, swore revenge on Pele, whom he felt was responsible for Lohi'au's death. He is credited with founding the "ancient, most renowned hula seminary of the island of Kaua'i, Ka Ulu a Paoa (the growth/ inspiration of Paoa)" (Kekahuna 1959). Today, the name Paoa remains a surname for Hawaiian families as well as for families in the southern islands below the equator, the islands from which Pele is believed to have come.

Kē'ē includes a small, difficult-to-navigate channel leading to the traditional canoe landing at what is now known as the "end of the road." A haven for canoes in antiquity and for small boats during the calm season well into historic times, John Hanohano Pā anchored his sampan there for long periods when he was fishing different areas in the *moku* of Nā Pali. Today, great numbers of tourists congregate there for snorkeling and sunbathing. Few are aware of the significance of this place to the Hawaiian people. State authorities, disregarding testimony from the Native people that the sand dunes there have for centuries been the resting place for the bones of the ancestors, built a leach field for public toilets there, displacing long-buried bones.

LAE O KA 'ĪLIO

Providing shelter from the wind to the canoe landing at Kē'ē, Lae o Ka 'Īlio (the headland of the dog) refers to the endangered Hawaiian monk seal known to Hawaiians as *'īlio hele i ka uaua* (dog running in the rough seas). Residents saw seals there even in the days before the federally established laws now protecting them caused a dramatic increase in their numbers in the main Hawaiian islands.

A conversation in 1986 about names along the Kalalau trail with Kaipo Chandler, longtime resident of Hā'ena, a hunter, fisherman, and cowboy there and who has worked and hunted in Nā Pali for most of his life (he is now in his eighties), brought to light information regarding whaling by Hawaiians in earlier times. He recalled that a point near Kē'ē high on the trail overlooking the sea was used as a lookout for whales during early historic times. Local whalers would row out in whaleboats, harpooning and killing the whale. They would then tow it back to Hanalei, where it would be butchered and rendered into oil.

Lae o Ka ʻĪlio. The endangered monk seal is known as ʻīlio hele i ka uaua *(dog running in the rough seas). Photograph by the U.S. Army, 1924, Bishop Museum.*

Hawaiians were excellent sailors, often recruited to sail on whalers during the early 1800s, the heyday of whaling in the Pacific. Although whaling from the beach is not spoken of much in the historic literature of Hawaiʻi, it is not inconceivable that these men brought back with them skills acquired on the whaling ships, using them to catch humpback whales during their yearly winter migration to Hawaiʻi and harvesting animals for food and/or profit. Some of the huge metal pots used for rendering whale blubber into oil are now museum pieces in Hanalei.

POHOLOKEIKI

Poholokeiki is a small channel just northeast of Lae O Ka ʻĪlio. *Poholo* means to sink, vanish, or disappear, and *keiki* means child or person. Though old-time fishermen conversant in the language of the land knew the meanings of the Hawaiian names, contemporary fishermen often do not, and English names have come to replace the Hawaiian ones. Upon learning the name of the channel meant sinking or vanishing child, one fisherman related a story about his own experience at the place that gives cause for those of us who frequent the sea to think about information the ancestors have left embedded in the names of places in Hāʻena and elsewhere.

This fisherman and his cousin set their nets out the evening before on the reef just to the windward side of Lae O Ka ʻĪlio, intending to pick them up in the morning, the usual practice for that type of fishing. As often happens during the winter season, a high surf came up suddenly in the night. In the morning, the tide was very low, and the reef was exposed during the lulls between large sets of waves. This should have made getting the nets much easier. However, mountainous waves coming in sets created an entirely different scenario. When the sets came hissing and roaring shoreward, water piled up onto and over the reef, sweeping away everything in its path and pouring into the tiny lagoon there. The powerful flood then raced seaward out the narrow channel, emptying out into the deep sea beyond the reef.

As nets can be a considerable investment, rather than let the surf destroy them completely, the two fishermen attempted to salvage them. One ran out onto the reef to retrieve the anchor securing the seaward end of the net, while his partner went for the shore side anchor, in close proximity to where the channel began. While the outside fisherman was trying to free the net, a large set of waves assaulted the reef. He was knocked down and swept to the edge of the channel, just managing to cling to the reef by sticking his fingers into holes of

Channel of vanishing children.
Limahuli Garden collection, 2002.

the living coral. Washed off his feet, he was dragged about three feet below the
surface as the water poured off the reef and into the channel. Luckily, the set
of waves did not last very long. The flow subsided before he ran out of breath.
Although he had cut his hands holding onto the coral in his struggle not to be
swept away, he survived to tell the story. As he got back to his feet and scrambled
back to the shore, he saw his cousin had also been knocked off his feet and held
underwater for a time. What saved him from being dragged out to sea was his
grip on the net anchor, which had been solidly secured to the reef near the beach.

PUʻUKAHUANUI

Puʻukahuanui is a reef fronting the area where Limahuli stream enters the sea,
two reefs to the east of Poholokeiki. *Puʻu* means small hump or rise, and Kahua
is the name of the sister of Lohiʻau, Pele's legendary lover. After Hiʻiaka restored
Lohiʻau's spirit to his body, his sister, Kahua, wanted to celebrate his recovery.
Hiʻiaka cautioned her that more time was needed to nurse him back to full health.
After two *anahulu*, each a ten-day Hawaiian "week," Lohiʻau was restored to full
health. His first priority was to go surfing with Hiʻiaka to celebrate his recovery.
Makaʻāinana from the district gathered on the shore joyously watching their
beloved *aliʻi* gracefully skimming the ocean waves with Hiʻiaka. Kahua then called
her *konohiki* and a great feast was prepared by the *makaʻāinana* for their *aliʻi*.

*Puʻukahuanui. Named after
his sister, Kahua, this reef
was possibly where Lohiau
and Hiʻiaka surfed together
to celebrate the restoration
of his spirit to his body.
Photograph by Hauʻoli
Wichman, 2007.*

This part of the Hiʻiaka story holds special interest for surfers today, for
Puʻukahuanui is still considered a quality surfing break. Only surfable at certain
times of the year, it is an especially challenging and temperamental spot. Breaking in shallow water, it is also one of the most hollow and powerful winter waves
in Hāʻena.

The next reef to the west is called Puʻukahuaiki (small Kahua). Both Puʻukahuanui and Puʻukahuaiki emerge above the water during the low tides marking the full and new moons. *Nui* (big) and *iki* (small) refer to the reefs' relative

heights. Since Puʻukahuanui is higher, it is above water longer in the incoming tide. This is important information for fishermen, who follow the rising water to catch the fish grazing on the *limu* (seaweed) growing there.

Thomas: Puʻukahuanui and Puʻukahuaiki. That's the ʻāpapa on two sides. Puʻu-kahuaiki? Puʻukahuaiki is the one ʻāpapa below Double-Ditch. You know when you come outside by Koia? Koia is the name of where the stream (Limahuli) drains into the ocean. Koia is right here, by the river mouth. We used to go over there go catch the mullet, eh. So the old man say "Eh, get one big pile mullet down Koia." So we know already, by the river mouth. Koia.

Okay, Puukahuaiki is the ʻāpapa that's on the right side of that river mouth. And Puʻukahuanui is the one on the left side. Sometimes the guys, they go surf around that bend that point. That whole ʻāpapa is Puʻukahuanui. Only the part sticking out here is Puʻukahuaiki? Puʻukahuaiki.

Violet: These ʻāpapa (reefs), they get name. Too bad when you folks came to gather information so late like this, my dad has gone. You know my dad knew every nook and cranny. They all have names, all these ʻāpapa get names. Uncle Tom knows some because that's where he went fishing with my dad and so my dad told him the names. Even like the ʻāpapa outside (in deeper water), all get certain, certain names. And Tom knows some of them. You know before we made up our own names, Rice ʻāpapa. It does have a Hawaiian name. We don't know the names, it's quite sad.

Renaming of the land and the loss of the old names are ongoing phenomena in the *ahupuaʻa* of Hāʻena, as in the rest of the world. Renewed commitment to the Hawaiian language and the return of young Hawaiians to the land, seeking as much as possible to practice ancestral customs and traditional skills, have begun, in some instances, to reverse the trend. The son of *kupuna* Mary Wann, an avid surfer, has returned to the land belonging to his family alongside Limahuli stream, just shoreward of Puʻukahuanui. His mother passed on to him a family name for the area including the reef and accompanying surf break. Kamealoha (the beloved) is now what friends and extended *ʻohana* (family) call the surf-break. Names are often treated as family heirlooms, passed from one generation to another. Restoring Hawaiian names for places and people is also a strategy used for reclaiming Hawaiian identity in these times of globalization and homogenizing of cultures. Sadly, Hawaiian names are also used in extremely inappropriate ways, as can be evidenced by a search of phone books under the word *aloha*, which has been appropriated by a variety of individuals and busi-nesses including but not limited to peddling automobiles, T-shirts, sheetmetal work, promises of sexual and marital bliss, and waste management systems.

*Lua'āweoweo
('Āweoweo hole).
No fisherman in
his right mind
would disclose the
exact location of
his fishing hole.
Suffice to say that
this hole is in the
deep waters outside
the sheltering reefs of
Makua. Photograph
by Air Survey
Hawai'i, 2002.*

KALUA'ĀWEOWEO

Of the many names given to places underwater in the outlying reefs of Hā'ena, we will look at one, the well-known Kalua'āweoweo.

Henry Gomes, a *kupuna* from Wainiha, another well known fisherman of Halele'a *moku,* preferred to fish alone for the most part. Very protective of his skills, he seldom showed people his fishing methods and gear. Even when well into his seventies, he still continued to fish alone at night in a sixteen-foot open runabout powered by two, small, 10 horsepower outboard engines. Departing at sunset from Hanalei Bay with a small cooler of beer, usually on nights around the time of the full moon, he would return in the dawn with the bottom of his boat strewn with empty aluminum cans, his cooler full of *'āweoweo* (various species of *Priacanthus*—bigeye). This red fish with large eyes and white flesh grows to about twenty inches long, and is very popular with Hawai'i's Asian community because of its tastiness and its lucky color. *'Āweoweo* usually stay in holes (*lua*) in the reef during the day, coming out to hunt for food at night.

Henry would often grumble about all of the newcomers moving into the area. He complained that these people were not only changing the names, they were also ruining the fishing, because they lacked the values of the old Hawaiians. Such people did not understand proper fishing behavior, and didn't care about conservation, taking and taking until only few or no fish remained. Kalua'āweoweo was a prime example, Henry said. This known *ko'a* (house) for the fish had always provided for the community during his youth. Now, he said, there weren't any more fish there, like there used to be.

He explained how the elders "fed" the fish. The ocean, he said, was like the land and the fish like people. Much of the ocean is only sparsely populated with desirable fish, because like people in their cities and towns, fish cluster together in desirable places and are not scattered evenly across the floor of the ocean. The ancestors knew these places, and called them *ko'a.* They also knew what species lived where as well as their individual habits and food. Fishermen throughout the world know these things. Hawaiians, who were described by early European explorers as being almost amphibious, were no different. They would visit *ko'a* and feed the fish even when they were not fishing, supplementing the natural food produced by the ocean with what they brought along from the land, thereby attracting fish from other areas into their *ko'a.* Henry continued this common-sense, utilitarian practice until he stopped fishing, shortly after the death of his wife. Henry passed away in the mid-1990s.

*Hawaiians, forever fond of traveling, visited
extended family in other* ahupuaʻa, *followed
yearly roundups, or merely went "holoholo."
Here a* hala *tree on the Hāʻena plain serves as
garage, clothesline, restaurant, and country
inn for a traveling party. Photograph by
Alfred Mitchell, 1892, Bishop Museum.*

CHAPTER THREE

FROM AHUPUAʻA TO REAL ESTATE

OVER THE APPROXIMATELY two thousand years people have inhabited these islands the land has changed. Due in large part to the isolated location of the islands in middle of the great ocean, these changes came slowly. Each time change came—brought by wind or tide or by early voyagers from the southern islands—a certain measure of equilibrium was eventually restored. In the last two hundred or so years, however, a flood of profound biological, economic, political, and social changes has been visited upon the islands, beginning with the arrival of Captain Cook in 1778. Often in staggering numbers and ranging in size from microbes to horses, cattle, and even elephants, the deluge has brought a multitude of new animals and plants, sometimes purposely, sometimes inadvertently. These changes have come with amazing rapidity as time and distance are shortened, many severely disturbing the balance established in the two thousand or so years preceding arrivals from Europe, the Americas, and Asia. This phenomenon continues at an even faster pace each day.

New ideas regarding social structures, religious beliefs, and government have been just as unsettling to the equilibrium of island ways. In all of Hawaiʻi, new perceptions regarding the responsibilities and appropriate relationships of the human population with the land have radically affected the people and altered forever the way they experience this unique place. Pressures exerted by places in the world far from the Hawaiian Islands have radically altered the traditional and customary relationship the people enjoyed with the land. This chapter documents the practices and life ways the aboriginal people evolved in order to fulfill their responsibilities to each other and *ʻāina,* their elder sibling and source of life, as they contended with and adjusted to these new elements whose sources came from faraway, foreign lands. The historic changes described herein affected all of Hawaiian society so the story told here will begin with what happened in the broader context of the history of Hawaiʻi, as these changes definitely had repercussions in Hāʻena.

In order to underscore how differently Hawaiians viewed these changes, this chapter contrasts and compares the terminology used by Euro-Americans to describe Hawaiian society to language aboriginal people used to describe themselves. These nuances of language demonstrate how differently, in many instances, the Native people perceived the changes that were wrought in their homeland. Another important contribution to understanding the changes that came about

69

in later years is to examine the traditional structure of society as seen through Hawaiian eyes.

KINGS, CHIEFS, AND COMMONERS

Though most histories written by foreigners describe Hawai'i as a feudal society (Kuykendall 1938: 269, 298; Alexander 1889: 4; Dougherty 1992: 20), there were fundamental differences between European feudal societies and the societal system existing in the Hawaiian Islands. In most cases, early Euro-Americans interpreted what they saw of Hawaiian society through the lenses of their own history and experience. They saw powerful individuals, the *mō'ī*, who seemed to dictate what happened in both the secular and religious sectors of life. They observed the populace prostrating themselves before these individuals, both men and women, who were treated almost as if they were gods walking among the people. They encountered many grades of warriors of formidable physical skill and their women, the *ali'i*, who led and coordinated activities of the populace in both peace and war. They were confronted by a religious system controlled by a powerful group of individuals, the *kahuna*, who directed rituals connecting people and the spiritual world. They were amazed at the energy and industry of the great majority of the population, the *maka'āinana*, who cultivated the land, performing the many tasks of horticulturalists, artisans, and technicians.

Defining the system they encountered in the islands in terms with which they were familiar, Euro-Americans called the *mō'ī* kings and queens. *Ali'i*, they named chiefs or lords. *Kahuna*, they labeled priests. *Maka'āinana*, who tilled the land, fished the seas, and gathered from mountaintop to ocean depths, they called commoners. Of course, when examined more closely, the workings of Hawaiian society were in fact very different from the society these adventurers and entrepreneurs had left behind in Europe and in the European colonized Americas.

It is understandable that these comparisons were made because the history of Europe and America was the foundation upon which Euro-Americans based the conclusions of all their observations. Perhaps they saw in the treatment of the *mō'ī* a reflection of the concept of the divine right kings in Europe were assumed to have. Perhaps the ability of the *ali'i* to direct the activities of large numbers of people in civic projects or engage them in war showed them to be similar to the lords who ruled the fiefdoms of Europe and large plantations of America. Certainly, the *kahuna* were impressive in their roles directing the rituals devoted to *akua* comparable to those of the robed priests, bishops, and other powerful clerics of the churches of Christianity. The great populace producing most of the food and goods led these foreigners to think that the *maka'āinana* were exactly like the serfs of Europe or the indentured servants of early America. In actuality, the dynamics of society in Hawai'i were not quite as early Euro-Americans and foreign historians described them.

MAKAʻĀINANA AND HOAʻĀINA

Perhaps the most marked difference between European feudal systems and the traditional and customary lifestyle of the Hawaiian people, especially as it impacted the largest segment of the population, was that *makaʻāinana* were neither bound to the land nor considered the property of lords (Lam 1989: 240). *Makaʻāinana* did not owe military service to the *aliʻi,* and their rights of access to the land and sea resources of their *ahupuaʻa* were long established and enabled them to provide for their own needs and ensure their own well-being. Although these rights were subject to the constraints of a system of *kapu* (rules regulating behavior) and the administration of *konohiki, makaʻāinana* retained a great measure of self-determination in contrast to the commoners and serfs enmeshed in European feudal systems (Lam 1985: 106).

When land documents of the Mahele period were translated into English, the word *commoner* or *tenant* replaced both the terms *hoaʻāina* and *makaʻāinana,* even though these people were far from common and were tenants only in the broadest sense of the word, as "dwellers in a place." The actual translation of the words as seen from a Hawaiian perspective presents a much different picture of the relationship these people had with each other and the land. One facet of the word *makaʻāinana* refers to those who dwelt or subsisted on the land—*ma* (at or on) *ka* (the) *ʻāinana* (that which is on the land). An alternate translation is *maka* (eyes or shoots) *ʻāinana* (that which is on the land). This is a reference to the eyes of the land (as in *maka,* also meaning emerging shoots in plant life) (Handy, Handy, and Pukui 1978: 323; Pukui and Elbert 1986: 224). Pukui states that *makaʻāinana* is a contraction of *lunamakaʻāinana,* meaning people that attend to the land or caring of the land (Pukui, Haertig, and Lee 1972: vol. 2, 287).

Another word translated as commoner or tenant is *hoaʻāina,* a term made up of two words: *hoa,* meaning friend, companion, and peer (Pukui and Elbert 1986: 73) and *ʻāina,* again a reference to the land or "that which feeds." The relationship between a friend or companion of the land contrasts sharply with the connotations attached to the words *commoner* and *tenant,* which refer to someone paying rent to use or occupy land, a building, or other property owned by another. Those emotional and familial ties binding the people and the land together, expressed in so many songs, sayings, and chants of the Hawaiian people, are entirely absent from the word *tenant.* Nor were the people on the land "common" in any sense of the word. *Makaʻāinana* had many specialized skills. They were healers, craftsmen, seamen, and horticulturists. They were adepts at animal husbandry, at managing game, and at managing fisheries that remained viable for centuries. These "commoners" practiced most of the skills that made for a prosperous subsistence society (Pukui, Haertig, and Lee 1972: vol. 2, 287; Handy, Handy, and Pukui 1978: 323).

The following is a self-description of a *makaʻāinana:*

I am makaʻāinana, a child of the land. No men prostrate themselves
before me; yet, I prostrate myself only before my aliʻi. My genealogy
is not chanted in the formal style of the chiefs; yet, I know from what
lineage I came. I am a plain man and humble, for that is proper. Yet
in my humility, I respect myself.

Pukui, Haertig, and Lee 1972: vol. 2, 286

Perhaps the term *freeholder* more accurately describes the relationship of the
makaʻāinana to the *ʻāina* and their role in the dynamics of life as practiced in
Hawaiian society. In traditional times, *makaʻāinana* did not own the land—
neither did *aliʻi* or *mōʻī*. *Makaʻāinana* had rights of access and use to land and
resources rare under contemporary regimes of government and barely understood
today in societies that subscribe to ideas of private property based on exclusion.

Under traditional customs and practices, *makaʻāinana* had extremely generous user rights that granted them access to the *waiwai* (wealth, resources) of the
land, extending from the tops of the mountains out into the depths of the surrounding sea (Lam 1985: 106). The user rights were of course regulated by socially
generated rules that have come to be called the *kapu* system, These rights were
not, however, derived from the authority of the *konohiki,* the *aliʻi,* or the *mōʻī,*
but were considered self-evident. Nor were the lines of authority hard and fast,
for some *makaʻāinana* were very uncommon indeed.

At the very top of Hawaiʻi's social system were the aliʻi. These were the
nīʻaupiʻo and piʻo, believed to be the direct descendants of the gods. Many
thought such aliʻi were themselves akua. Sacrosanct among the already
venerated was the piʻo, born of the brother-sister union of nīʻaupiʻo rank.
Here, sacred lineage was intact. No lesser ancestry diluted the mana
(power and authority) that came from gods to living piʻo. These chiefs
paid dearly for the privileges of high position. So sacred were they that
some could not even venture forth during the day, for all who saw them
must prostrate themselves immediately. Ranking below these high-ranking
aliʻi were approximately eight other gradations of rank, all arrived at by
genealogy. A bit separate from these ranks was an additional provision for
the rugged, but royal, individualist. This was the aliʻi makaʻāinana. Some
from among the nīʻaupiʻo, piʻo and naha [also extremely sacred] lived in
the country, keeping secret their aliʻi kapu [sacred status] and living like
ordinary people. Thus aliʻi families were among the makaʻāinana."

Pukui, Haertig, and Lee 1972: vol. 2, 286–287

Hawaiian society was established upon a foundation made up of the *makaʻāinana*.

ALIʻI

The term *aliʻi* is variously translated into English as chief(ess), officer, ruler, monarch, peer, headman, noble, aristocrat, king, queen, commander, royal, regal, and kingly. Most of these words have a feudal air about them—and perhaps also a dose of what Stannard (1991: 383) calls political mythology, the tendency of colonizing nations to describe indigenous people in derogatory terms as a way to justify the taking over of their countries. While words like *king, aristocrat,* and *monarch* might not seem disparaging on the face of it, when viewed from an American perspective, these terms identify institutions that, from a democratic perspective, should be replaced by more egalitarian institutions. The eradication of the Hawaiian chiefs, the kings, and the feudal kingdom newcomers would carry out in a little more than fifty years after they first arrived therefore becomes an admirable act of democratization, anointing its perpetrators as champions of the people.

If, however, we look to other sources of information offered by scholars of the Hawaiian language, we discover alternative meanings of the term *aliʻi* found in Hawaiian *ʻōlelo noʻeau* (sayings of wisdom) regarding this group of people. One of these epithets, *nāʻau aliʻi* (character of *aliʻi*), suggests a figure who is kind, thoughtful, forgiving, loving, beneficent, benevolent, and possessed of aloha (Pukui and Elbert 1986: 257). Americans founded their country by rejecting kings, lords, and landed aristocracy. *Aliʻi* could only be an anathema to these antiroyalists. For Native Hawaiians, though, good *aliʻi* were expected to be benevolent but firm elder siblings to the people.

From a Hawaiian viewpoint, *aliʻi* and *makaʻāinana* were the same people. *Makaʻāinana* living in *ahupuaʻa* felt an actual kinship to *aliʻi* as their relatives. The early Native Hawaiian historians Malo and Kamakau both state that *aliʻi* and *makaʻāinana* were one people descended from Papa and Wākea, with *aliʻi* coming from within the pool of people known as *makaʻāinana* (Kimura 1983: 182). The relationship between the two was an extension of those social customs based upon *ʻohana* (family) folkways. While not all *aliʻi* were paragons of virtue, this *ʻohana* relationship was the standard by which *aliʻi* were measured:

> In Hawaiʻi's past, the *ʻohana* authority and teachings were apparently supplemented and reinforced by a powerful law-making, law-enforcing control outside the family. This was the *aliʻi*. The loved, respected and obeyed *aliʻi* were apparently the rule; the cruel *aliʻi*, one abandoned or murdered, the exception. Thus, the Hawaiian had both *ʻohana* and *aliʻi* as group superegos and as models for behavior.
>
> Pukui, Haertig, and Lee 1972: vol. 2, 233

The relationship between the *maka'āinana* and his family and the *ali'i* was a very personal one, with ardent affection the prevailing feeling unless an *ali'i* was quite despicable, which Hawaiian sources say was rare in traditional times. *Ali'i* and *maka'āinana* were kinship terms, with *ali'i* being the equivalent of *kaikua'ana* (elder sibling). The Hawaiian language affirms this through the "O" class possessive markers in the language characteristic of kin relationships. *Ali'i* refer to *maka-'āinana* as *ko'u* (my) *maka'āinana*. *Maka'āinana* refer to *ali'i* as *ko'u* (my) *ali'i*. In contrast, "A" class markers, usually linked to material goods, also governed hired hands (*ka'u limahana*—my co-worker), wives (*ka'u wahine*—my wife), and even children (*ka'u keiki*—my children), indicating a less intimate bond (Kimura 1983: 183). Good *ali'i* were looked upon as revered and venerated senior relatives (Handy, Handy, and Pukui 1972: 326). When *ali'i* misused their powers and *kapu* responsibilities, they were removed by the group, and replaced—a practice for which there is ample evidence in Hawaiian traditions (Kimura 1983: 184).

Although *konohiki* and *ali'i* tend to get lumped together, the distinct roles each played in traditional society need to be understood to see how the imposition of Euro-American values on Hawaiian society affected traditional relationships with the land. For example, all *ali'i* were not *konohiki*, although most, if not all, *konohiki* could have been *ali'i*, given the many gradations of rank within the *ali'i* segment of society (Malo 1951: 80–81).

KONOHIKI

The Hawaiian dictionary says that a *konohiki* is a headman (or headwoman) of an *ahupua'a* land division, under the *ali'i*. Land or fishing rights under the control of the *konohiki* are also sometimes called *konohiki* rights (Pukui and Elbert 1986). However, by breaking the word down into its component parts, one can expand the dictionary definition, showing how wide-ranging and important the role of *konohiki* was in traditional *ahupua'a* society. *Kono* means to invite, entice, induce, or prompt. The term *hiki* commonly conveys the idea that something can be done, that it is within the realm of the possible. Handy, Handy, and Pukui (1972: 321–322) write that *konohiki* were relatives of the ruling *ali'i*, appointed to supervise the distribution of land, to coordinate planting and harvesting, to mediate water rights, and to organize the building and maintenance of irrigation ditches and the construction of new *lo'i* (complexes of irrigation channels and pondfields for planting taro). In consultation with *maka'āinana*, *konohiki* also enforced seasonal *kapu* protecting various kinds of fish during spawning seasons and supervising the distribution of the catch from communal fishing ventures in the deep ocean and in those waters that were part of each *ahupua'a* fishery.

During the *makahiki* (a type of annual harvest festival), *konohiki* made sure that *ho'okupu* (gifts for fostering growth) and *'auhau* (tribute to elevated *ali'i* genealogies) were offered in the right quantities and quality to *kahuna* (ritual specialists) and to the entourage accompanying the *akua lono* (god of peace and agriculture) in its procession around the island each year. In historic times, after capitalism had been introduced to Hawai'i, *konohiki* were often transformed into tax collectors, landlords, and even game wardens for certain fisheries. The result is that a number of Hawaiians still view *konohiki* operating under newer forms of government inspired by Euro-American notions as overbearing and oppressive rather than as facilitators and communicators who looked out for the overall interests of the people.

In traditional society, people met their entire material and spiritual needs by drawing from the land and sea within and around the islands. Food, crops, products of their manufacture, or labor fulfilled their obligations to each other and to the governing structure. With the entry of Euro-Americans and introduction of their values, the daily functioning of island society came to depend more and more on cash and the market economy. As the Native people lost access to land and resources, even the most basic needs of food, clothing, and shelter came to be met by imported goods. This dependence has become so extreme that if today the islands were shut off from the rest of the world for a somewhat longer than usual length of time, perhaps for reasons resembling the aftermath of the September 11, 2001 tragedies or natural disasters like the New Orleans hurricane-inflicted gas crisis of 2005, within weeks there would be extreme difficulty in island society, if not outright chaos.

In pre-European times, all segments of island society were entirely interdependent. Sources for livelihood and the resources available for use by the people were all contained within the environs of the islands. By today's standards these resources were very basic but they were sufficient for the ancestors to have a full and meaningful life as long as they fulfilled their mutual responsibilities to each other and the *'āina*. *Konohiki* therefore had to possess a wide array of skills. They had to know all of the *waiwai* (assets) contained within each *ahupua'a*—hydrologic, biologic, and geologic. They had to know the state of the soil, plants, and animals on land and sea, and guide decisions on their use. Most important, *konohiki* had to know how to deal with human beings.

In traditional society, *konohiki* were bridges connecting the governing and the governed. *Konohiki* had to gather in the fruits of *ahupua'a* for *ali'i, mō'ī,* and *akua*. However, they needed to ensure that the producers of these fruits, the *maka'āinana,* were well cared for and fairly treated. If not, according to traditional custom and practices, *maka'āinana* were free to move and invest their time and energy under more deserving *konohiki*—an option easily made possible by the extensive kinship networks enjoyed by most families extending far outside a single *ahupua'a* (Lam 1989: 240). Given this freedom of movement enjoyed by *makaʻāinana, konohiki* had to be experts at "inviting" both *makaʻāinana* and *aliʻi* to participate in tasks necessary to preserve order and prosperity within their *ahupuaʻa*. In addition, *konohiki* also had to have respect from the people and enough charisma to draw in and make *makaʻāinana* feel confidence about investing their lives and energy in the long-term success of the *ahupuaʻa*.

MŌʻĪ

Mōʻī is a word of more recent origin. Pukui and Elbert (1986) define it as king, sovereign, monarch, majesty, ruler, queen, and related to the word *ʻī*, meaning supreme. J.F.G. Stokes claims that the word *mōʻī* first appeared in print in 1832 (in Pukui and Elbert 1986). According to Fornander, both Kepelino (1932) and Kamakau (n.d.) said that *mōʻī* were a rank of *aliʻi* who could succeed to government, but were of lower rank than *aliʻi* descended from the god Kāne (Fornander 1999). Kameʻeleihiwa (1992) relates that *aliʻi nui* (*mōʻī*) were mediators between the divine and the human, placating and manipulating those more dangerous and unseen *akua* whose powers regulated the earth and all the awesome forces of nature. In missionary and other foreigners' writings, *mōʻī* (and *aliʻi*) are often portrayed as being ineffective, despotic, and decadent (Kuykendall 1938: 89). This is not surprising given the connotations the English word *king* had for these writers: the European feudal system, with its socioeconomic stratification and distance, and the historical American rebellion against King George of England.

ʻĀINA

The people of Hawaiʻi perceived themselves as younger siblings of the *ʻāina*, the islands, which provided nourishment for body, mind, and spirit. From the earliest encounters, foreigners saw the Hawaiian Islands as valuable places to restock their ships and as places where their crews could find recreation and diversion after long, tiring journeys. Other visitors soon saw the islands as promising new territory for accumulating wealth. These included fortune-hunting entrepreneurs as well as representatives of nation-states seeking to enrich the coffers of their treasuries and acquire territory for their empires.

The word *ʻāina* means far more than the simplistic English term *land* suggests. Derived from the term *ʻai* (food, to eat) or more broadly, "that which feeds or nourishes," *ʻāina* goes far beyond the material feeding of the physical body. As illustrated by the stories of places linking *akua* like Pele, Kāne, and Kanaloa and the other spiritual beings to the land, *ʻāina* also refers to the nourishment of mind and spirit. The dual aspects of spirit and mind remain inseparable from Native understandings of *ʻāina*, which nourish Hawaiian identity, and mystically and genealogically connect the people to the islands and to generations of ancestors who came before them. This understanding of *ʻaina* is critical to the continued well-being of the Hawaiian people. The concept embraces much more than simply land or real estate.

As long as traditional Hawaiian relationships with the land survived, however, newcomers had to depend on Native goodwill to gain or hold land, since the islands were held in common by all of the people. Most foreigners wanted to hold land as private property, not subject to the ways of what they considered a primitive people who saw the world very differently from those whose roots were still in Europe and Euro-colonized America.

Pre-European systems of governance in Hawai'i had produced a healthy, industrious populace and time-tested methods for sustaining resources for centuries. Now Native Hawaiians were being told by their newly arrived Euro-American friends that they needed to change their government so it would more closely resemble those existing in the rest of the world in order to survive and be recognized by the more enlightened nations. They were also told that that change was especially necessary at a time when predatory imperial powers were casting a wide net in the Pacific, collecting territories to add to their colonial portfolios. In the mid-1800s, then, the leaders of the Hawaiian people began the task of constructing a new form of government, guided by missionaries and other advisors from Europe and America, to fulfill their expectations and protect their nation from assault. The result was the development of a constitutional monarchy, with an executive branch, occupied by the *mō'ī;* a legislative branch, made up of two houses, a House of Nobles and House of Representatives; and a judicial branch.

The issue at the core of most conflicts between Natives and foreigners in the years preceding the enacting of legislation beginning the process of privatization of land was the possession of land. Foreigners applied constant pressure on the fledgling Hawaiian government to grant them land for their various business and entrepreneurial activities. In response to these pressures and under the tutelage of foreign advisors, the new government of Hawai'i passed legislation transforming traditional society and its practices, especially land use. The *mō'ī,* once perceived as an *akua* walking among men acting as a conduit of *mana* (spiritual power) from the gods, was transformed by this process into an executive of government. The positions of both *ali'i,* traditionally closest advisors to the *mō'ī* on matters of government and politics, and *kahuna,* traditional advisors to the *mō'ī* and to the people on matters of skill and knowledge in both the spiritual and natural worlds, were slowly replaced by a new code of written law, subject to the influence of men of property.

Because of these changes, the *maka'āinana* gradually lost access to *ahupua'a,* where they once gained their subsistence and fulfilled their private obligations (personal and family) and their public responsibilities (contributions to government and community) entirely by the fruits of their labor on the land in which they lived. Lines drawn, recorded, registered, and filed away in central offices worked to fracture and fragment their world. These calamitous changes eventually forced the *makaʻāinana* to become a pool of cheap labor, transformed into pawns in games of profit and accumulation directed and scripted in cities and countries far across the ocean.

CHANGING RELATIONSHIPS, RIGHTS, AND RESPONSIBILITIES

In the early years of the Hawaiian nation, newly imported ideas about land and the accompanying expectations of foreigners provoked confusion and conflict, not only between newcomers, the Hawaiian government, and the populace, but also between different elements within the Native Hawaiian community. To preserve peace and to accommodate the growing influx of newcomers and their ideas, the fledgling government enacted laws that would forever change the face of the land. During this critical juncture of history the *mōʻī* struggled to carry out his role as leader and protector of the Hawaiian people while at the same time dealing with situations never before faced by his predecessors.

In 1839, Kauikeouli, Kamehameha III proclaimed a Declaration of Rights guaranteeing protection to "all people, together with their lands, their building lots and all their property." According to this law, "nothing whatever shall be taken from any individual, except by express provision of the laws" (Kuykendall 1938: 112–122). In the following year, the Constitution of 1840 formally declared that the land belonged to the chiefs and people, with the king as trustee for all:

> *O Kamehameha I, ʻo ia ke poʻo o kēia aupuni, a nona nō nā ʻāina a pau mai Hawaiʻi ā Niʻihau, ʻaʻole naʻe nona ponoʻī, no nā kanaka nō, a me nā aliʻi, a ʻo Kamehameha nō kō lākou poʻo nāna e ʻōlelo i ka ʻāina*
> Laws of His Majesty Kamehameha III 1841: 4; Laws of His Majesty Kamehameha III 1842: 11–12

> *Kamehameha the first was the founder the kingdom, and to him belonged all the land from one end of the Islands to the other,* although it was not his own private property. It belonged to the chiefs and people in common, of whom Kamehameha I was the head, and had the management of the landed property.
> Thurston 1904: 3, emphasis added

This Constitution, and the laws enacted immediately after, tried to end conflicts between Hawaiians and foreigners (Kuykendall 1938: 273–298) yet retain the design of the traditional land system. Land could not be conveyed without the consent of the *mō'ī*. More often than not, however, the laws seemed designed primarily to appease foreign interests. For example, one constitutional provision was interpreted to mean that the crown would not reclaim land already held by foreigners (Thurston 1904: 1; Hawaiian Constitution preamble, 1840). Another law allowed various island governors to grant fifty-year leases to foreigners, a concession that foreigners, astonishingly, looked upon as an attempt to deprive them of their rights! In response to a letter from the American consul, the *mō'ī* explained his position and that of his people:

> At the present time we have adopted new views in relation to the premises occupied by foreigners. We lay no claims whatever to any property of theirs, either growing, or erected on the soil. That is theirs exclusively. We simply claim the soil itself, but do not claim that even that should be restored, though from of old we have never had the smallest idea of alienating any portion of our land. But if the soil be not restored, then we claim a reasonable rent.
> Kuykendall 1938: 276

Despite this apparently reasonable request, foreigners were bent upon acquiring permanent toeholds for capitalist endeavor, and looked for military backing from countries whose imperialistic motives were obvious (Kuykendall 1938: 177). As a result of this pressure, this inequality of power, and this intractable conflict, a new voice arose in the discourse of social interaction in Hawai'i, one displaying all the latent belligerence underlying the culture of accumulation, boiling to the surface whenever its will was thwarted, then as now.

To address the growing problem of foreign desires for Native land, an 1845 law established a Board of Land Commissioners to investigate, and then to approve or reject, all claims by private individuals, whether Natives or foreigners, to land acquired prior to the creation of the commission. Since the interests of *mō'ī, ali'i,* and *maka'āinana* in the lands of Hawai'i were so intertwined and indivisible, the commission could not at first act on the bulk of the claims, handling only a small number during the first few years. And yet, even though fee simple ownership was not yet part of the Hawaiian legal system, the commission issued fee patents on these awards. With this development, the commission blatantly ignored the idea of the *'āina* as the elder sibling to the Hawaiian people conveyed in the Kumulipo and the land began its transformation into real estate. *'Āina* that had fed the Hawaiian people's bodies, minds, and spirits, *'aina* that had been family to the Hawaiian people, had begun to be privatized.

LANDLORDS AND TENANTS

Because it was the best, most sheltered harbor in the islands at the time, Honolulu had become headquarters for the government of the new Hawaiian nation. This meant that most discussions leading to legislation that redefined the relationships between the people and the land took place far away from relatively isolated places on neighbor islands like Hāʻena. But the legislation eventually affected all parts of the Hawaiian nation and, while the changes came more slowly in the outlying district, they came nevertheless.

In 1846, the Land Commission adopted seven principles to guide their work in determining land ownership. The commission identified three classes of persons as having vested rights in the land: the government (*mōʻī*), the landlord (*aliʻi* and/or *konohiki*), and the tenant (*makaʻāinana/hoaʻāina*). The first five principles identified the kind and degree of proof necessary for people desiring to file a claim for land. The sixth set a commutation due to the government at one-third and recognized the rights of the tenants (Revised Laws 1925, 2126). This commutation was a kind of tax whereby the government would receive one-third of the value of the land in either land or currency. The recognition of the rights of the tenants will be discussed more fully later in this story. The seventh principle "emphatically declared that anyone not filing a claim with the Land Commission on or before February 14, 1848 forfeited his interest in the land to the government" (Chinen 1958: 12).

This codifying of the people's relationship to the land as shown in early government documents of the fledgling Hawaiian nation was to become primary in determining how Native people related to each other and to their world from that point onward. Since foreign advisors convinced the *mōʻī* that land dispositions and decisions should be governed by foreign rules instead of Hawaiian custom, language came to play an exceedingly important role in this transformation. This was especially important when the English language gained legal ascendancy over Native language in the later history of Hawaiʻi (Merry 2000: 103).

LAW, THE NEW KAPU

The Mahele of 1848 and the Kuleana Act of 1850 were two of the most important pieces of legislation marking the change from traditional, communal use of *ʻāina* to ownership of land as private property. After debating land issues for almost two years, the *mōʻī* and *aliʻi* accepted a plan drafted by Justice William Lee. The *mōʻī* would retain his private lands "subject only to the rights of the tenants." The rest of the land would be divided into thirds: one-third to the Hawaiian government, one-third to the *aliʻi* (*konohiki*), and one-third to the *makaʻāinana*, "the actual possessors and cultivators of the soil" (Privy Council Records). By the time the legislation was actually enacted, however, the *mōʻī*, the government, and the *aliʻi*

William Hyde Rice sits with an unidentified
Hawaiian man while visiting Hāʻena. Rice's
descendants later came to own considerable
landholdings in Hāʻena. Known to be a friend
to the people, he and certain members of his
family were trusted and looked to for leadership
in matters concerning the new Euro-American
influenced regime that had transformed the
land. Photograph by Alfred Mitchell, 1892,
Bishop Museum.

(konohiki) possessed the bulk of the land between them (Kuykendall 1938). The maka'āinana did not fare so well.

> It is estimated that of the 8,205 awards given by the Land Commission, 7,500 awards included kuleana lands [awarded to maka'āinana and lesser ali'i]. This resulted, however, in only 26 percent of the adult male native population receiving such lands. The plan adopted by the king and chiefs for division of the land had stated that the maka'āinana were to receive, after the king partitioned out his personal lands, one third of the land of Hawai'i. However, only 28,000 acres, much less than one percent of the total land went to the maka'āinana.
> MacKenzie 1991: 8

The mō'ī, the major ali'i, and the government had separated out their individual interests by quitting their claims to each other, dividing the lands of Hawai'i between them in what came to be called by some the "Great" Mahele of 1848. However, it was not until the Kuleana Act of 1850 that maka'āinana claims would be considered. One phrase—"koe wale no na kuleana o na kanaka e noho ana ma ua aina la" (reserving only the right of the people who live on the aforementioned land)—was embedded in the deeds of almost all of the lands disbursed in the Mahele. This articulation of the rights of the people in Hawaiian law is extremely important, for it distinguishes Hawaiian land laws from the land laws of most of the rest of the continental United States. This element of the law embedded in the foundational documents defining property in Hawai'i remains controversial to this day, a result of differing perceptions of how people should relate to 'āina.

INTENT

What the mō'ī, Kamehameha III, tried to do during the time when the laws restructuring land tenure were enacted was to safeguard his people's way of life and to keep Hawai'i from being overrun by the predatory nations of France, Great Britain, the Netherlands, Germany, and the United States, who were absorbing other islands and lands in the Pacific (Merry 2000: 90–91; Chinen 1958: 25). He assumed these newly enacted laws would protect maka'āinana, allowing them to make an adequate livelihood by exercising their traditional use rights within the system of customs that had been practiced on ahupua'a lands during the preceding centuries.

He also apparently believed a mixed legal system could combine a fee simple regime for fields in cultivation with a traditional regime of gathering, hunting, and fishing for residents on undeveloped lands within the ahupua'a (Lam 1985:

119). Kamehameha III believed that, by recording titles, Hawaiians could forever secure their *ʻāina*. What he did not foresee was that these foreigners, whose ideas of the land did not include preserving forever the basic needs of the Hawaiian way of life, would eventually take his country from the people. These foreigners saw land as the means to increase their fortunes and to solidify their place in the islands. They set about replacing the Hawaiian worldview with a vision imported from continental America and Europe.

> *The Kuleana Act, in the language of law, listed the resources available to makaʻāinana. When the landlords have taken allodial titles to their lands, the people on each of their lands shall not be deprived of the right to take firewood, house timber, aho cord, thatch, or ti leaf, from the land on which they live, for their private use, should they need them, but they shall not have the right to take such articles to sell for profit. The people shall also have a right to drinking water, and running water, and roads shall be free to all, should they need them, on all lands granted in fee simple: provided, that this shall not be applicable to wells and water courses which individuals have made for their own use.*
> Hawaii Revised Statutes, section 7.1

Kamehameha III specifically asked that this provision be appended to the Kuleana Act because he recognized that a little bit of land, even with allodial title, would be of very little value if the owners were cut off from all other means of producing a livelihood. But ever since the enactment of these two primary pieces of legislation, lawsuits (brought mostly by foreigners) have challenged and attacked this right of *makaʻāinana* to continue to draw upon *ahupuaʻa* resources for their survival. As recently as 1982, in the case of *Kalipi v. Hawaiian Trust,* while the judgment sweepingly reconfirmed the traditional rights of *makaʻāinana* and re-anchored them on *ahupuaʻa* occupancy, it also made these rights subordinate to the "modern understanding of property" if and when the exercise of traditional rights disrupts that understanding (Lam 1985: 119).

The struggle continues. In October 2000, Patrick Barrett, formerly of California but now living in Mōʻiliʻili, Oʻahu, sued to challenge the constitutionality of Native Hawaiian gathering rights (among other things), citing the Equal Protection Clause of the Fourteenth Amendment to the U.S. Constitution. On July 12, 2001, the court dismissed the suit on a technicality, but Barrett, then fifty-three and on full medical disability with the Social Security Administration, said he would continue his mission. Colonialism is not in the past!

The Mahele (1848) was the vehicle by which the *mōʻī* and the *aliʻi* separated out their individual interests in the land. In the Mahele, all the lands of Hawaiʻi were divided between the *mōʻī* and *aliʻi* recorded in the Mahele Book. The *mōʻī* quitclaimed his interest in specific lands to a select group of *aliʻi* and these *aliʻi* quitclaimed their interests in the balance of the lands to the *mōʻī*. This did not confer title on the *aliʻi,* but merely acknowledged neither had claims to these specific lands, the *mōʻī* to the certain lands of the *aliʻi* and the *aliʻi* to the lands of the *mōʻī*. The transactions provided a basis for the privatization to come and was also the vehicle for the appearance of a new landholding entity: the government. The *mōʻī* then set apart approximately 1.5 million acres for the remaining *aliʻi* and the people (*makaʻāinana*). Later in the year, the legislative council accepted the lands, declaring them to be lands of the Hawaiian government, subject always to the rights of the tenants (Laws of Kamehameha III 1840) and became a major landholder itself in the process of privatization. This government later exacted fees from *makaʻāinana* and *aliʻi* alike. Fees were collected from *makaʻāinana* registering claims for land the government deemed appropriate to grant them under the Kuleana Act (1850). *Aliʻi* paid commutations to the government of one-third the value of land, or conveyed land itself upon confirmation of lands divided by quitclaim in the process of the Mahele.

During this phase of privatization of the land, *makaʻāinana* had to register claims if they wanted to legally own land they had been occupying for generations. However, due to a variety of factors, relatively few *makaʻāinana* submitted claims and even fewer were awarded lands. As a result, far less than one percent of the land in Hawaiʻi was awarded to the people who actually worked the land. Several of the reasons given by historians and observers of the time are as follows.

Many *makaʻāinana* were not aware of the importance of owning their land having never experienced this unfamiliar practice that contrasted sharply with life ways in the past centuries. No one explained to them that, should they fail to obtain their own lands and should the *aliʻi* or *konohiki* later lease or sell *ahupuaʻa* lands on which their homes were located, new owners could evict the *makaʻāinana* from their homes. Another reason was that the timeline was unrealistic. The new laws provided only two years for the people to register their claims. One Hawaiian writer at the time said that it would have been much more appropriate if the time was twenty years.

Another reason given was the government's failure to inform a population still ill at ease with the written word. Still another factor was the lack of money. *Makaʻāinana,* especially those in the outlying districts away from the port towns, had very limited access to cash. They could ill afford the survey fees required for submitting and receiving awards of land. Most important, however, was the fear that by taking an award, *makaʻāinana* might be limiting their own access to the *waiwai* (resources) of the *ahupuaʻa,* simply because the restrictions required by the claim and the survey seemed the opposite of traditional access to the entire *ahupuaʻa* (Lam 1985: 112). It is entirely plausible that some *makaʻāinana* assumed that if they did not act to change anything, the traditional system would simply continue. Also, there is some evidence to support the possibility that those living under less than honorable *konohiki* were compelled not to file claims or feared reprisals if they filed a claim (Lam 1989: 263; Chinen 2006: 9).

The Mahele and the Kuleana Act also forever altered the traditional relationships between *mōʻī, aliʻi,* and *makaʻāinana.* The *mōʻī,* once connected by genealogy to *akua,* became an abstraction called the "crown," a secular entity. *Aliʻi,* once expected to be kind, generous, and beloved leaders (Kimura 1983: 182–184), were transformed into landlords, and *ʻāina,* elder sibling, now seen through the eyes of the surveyor's glassy-eyed instrument and articulated in roods, rods, chains and acres, was no longer recognizable if not actually cultivated or built upon.

The loaded term *landlord,* with its roots in European feudal society, having a whole set of negative connotations still resonating in contemporary life along with new laws, when interpreted through the lens of Euro-American jurisprudence would eventually work to severely constrain the freedom of *makaʻāinana* to move at will throughout the *ahupuaʻa,* limiting access to the available resources of the land. The word *tenants* caged them within lines drawn in the surveys of their *kuleana* (lands awarded in the Kuleana Act a.k.a. Land Commission Awards) allowing them only the land they had under cultivation at the time of the survey and a house lot of no more than a quarter of an acre (MacKenzie 1991: 8).

The English words *crown, government, landlord,* and *tenant* defined new relationships of people to the land and to each other, as such words came to dominate all legal discussions regarding land in the years that followed. This is especially true when *makaʻāinana/hoaʻāina* were transformed by language into tenants. A tenant, in the Euro-American sense of the word, is commonly someone renting space from someone else (a landlord) or from another entity in possession of that space. Often in debt to the permanent owner of the land, tenants know that if the landlord forecloses, they will simply have to go. As we saw earlier, the translation of the term *makaʻāinana* (or *hoaʻāina*) defines a starkly different relationship. As will be shown, the Mahele and Kuleana Act had a profound and personal impact on the people of Hāʻena.

A neat and orderly interior of a Native house in Hāʻena. Hawaiian elders were, and continue to be, very fastidious about cleanliness and orderliness in all that they do. Photograph by Alfred Mitchell, 1892, Bishop Museum.

CHAPTER FOUR

THE IMPACT OF THE MAHELE AND KULEANA ACT

 IN THE MAHELE, Hāʻena was awarded to Abner Pākī, a powerful *aliʻi* closely allied with the Kamehameha family. Kamehameha III and approximately 250 *aliʻi* quitclaimed and separated out their interests in the lands of Hwaiʻi in the Mahele of 1848. The *mōʻī* kept approximately one million acres as his personal lands. The combined total of the 250 or so *aliʻi* was approximately 1,600,000 acres and the newly formed government of the nation of Hawaiʻi acquired approximately one-and-a-half million acres by the time the Mahele was complete. Significantly, almost all of the lands were granted and confirmed in deeds inscribed with the phrase "subject to the rights of the people," as mentioned previously.

Mahele lands were granted without survey or boundaries established by Western standards of metes and bounds. These lands were granted in "name alone," meaning transactions only required registration of the names of the lands. Like many important *aliʻi* closely associated with the Kamehameha family, Pākī received lands on several islands although he lived in Honolulu, close to the center of government.

ABNER PĀKĪ, ALIʻI

Abner Pākī received Hāʻena *ahupuaʻa* prior to the official Mahele (Privy Council Minutes, vol. 3, 373). He later (see Privy Council Records, vol. 3B, 539–544 [March 6, 1850], Hawaiʻi State Archives) reestablished his claim to the entire *ahupuaʻa* under a Land Commission Award (L.C.A. 10613). As mentioned, like most lands granted to *aliʻi*, this award was subject to the rights of the *makaʻāinana*.

Pākī was the grandson of the former Maui *mōʻī*, Kamehamehanui, who was the brother of Kahekili, the great Maui *aliʻi nui*. Pākī was married to the *aliʻi wahine* (female *aliʻi*) Konia, a daughter of the Kamehameha clan. Their child, Bernice Pauahi Bishop, would receive many lands from dying, childless *aliʻi* in the coming years. Eventually, these lands would comprise a massive estate she left to establish the Kamehameha Schools, a school for Native children. The act of leaving her estate to benefit the Hawaiian people was characteristic of *aliʻi* behavior, as we have seen. Other *aliʻi* did the same. Liliʻuokalani left her estate for the support of Hawaiian orphans; Lunalilo established a home for aging Hawaiians; and Emma founded Queen's Hospital (present-day Queen's Medical Center). Although protected by law, several of the trusts set up by the *aliʻi* are under legal assault by Americans intent on asserting constitutional law pertaining to racial discrimination.

| | Lands Awarded to Abner Pākī in the Mahele of 1848 | | |
| | Ko Abenera Paki | | |
Na Aina	Ahupuaa	Kalana	Mokupuni
Heeia	Ahupuaa	Koolau Poko	Oahu
Waialae	Ili no Waikiki	Kona	Oahu
Hanaloa	Ili no Waipio	Ewa	Oahu
Makaha	Ahupuaa	Waianae	Oahu
Haena	Ahupuaa	Halelea	Kauai
Puunau	Ahupuaa	Lahaina	Maui

Ke ae aku nei au i keia mahele, ua maikai. No Abenera Paki ka aina i kakau ia maluna: ua ae ia 'ku e hiki ke lawe aku imua o ka Poe Hoona Kuleana.

Hale Alii   *Kamehameha*
11, Febe. 1848

Pākī was an *ali'i* in the old tradition (Kame'eleihiwa 1992: 32). He resisted being Christianized, and together with Liliha, the widow of O'ahu Governor Boki and the guardian of Kamehameha III, represented the last vestiges of the old Native order. He displayed characteristics of traditional *konohiki*. One example of his ability to "invite" *ahupua'a* occupants to get a task done was the construction of an *'auwai* (irrigation canal) to supply a *lo'i* complex in Nu'uanu valley on O'ahu. The project was completed in three days by several hundred men. The aqueduct, known as Pākī *'auwai*, still carries water today. Pākī understood managing land, water resources, and people, and how to enhance them. Charismatic and firm in executing strategies for improving land and water systems, he was a favorite of Kamehameha III and was known for his great strength and distinguished appearance (Kamakau 1992: 298).

Letters from Pākī to the Department of Interior illustrate how Native perceptions and practices regarding land continued during this time of transition. In one of these proclamations, Pākī announced to the populace and the government that as *konohiki* he had reserved (*ho'omalu*) the *he'e* (octopus) as his protected "fish" within the fishery attached to the *ahupua'a* of Hā'ena. In other *ahupua'a* on Kaua'i awarded to him, he reserved *'uhu* (parrotfish—Lumaha'i *ahupua'a* in Halele'a) and *akule* (big-eyed scad—Wailua *ahupua'a, moku* of Puna). By documenting these protected fish in writing, Pākī, *ali'i,* proclaimed his traditional role as head administrator of the *ahupua'a* even under the new system of law.

OLELO HOʻOLAHA [NOTICE]
E haʻi aku nei au i nā iʻa Hoʻomalu ma nā ʻāina ponoʻī o
(I declare and reserve the [following] fish in my own lands.)

A. Paki.

HĀʻENA, KAUAʻI—HEʻE
LUMAHAʻI—ʻUHU
WAILUA—AKULE

Letter dated January 24, 1854, Interior Department Land File, State Archives

The word *hoʻomalu* used in this proclamation is also significant. As translated above, one definition is reserve, with a connotation of ownership. But an alternative meaning for the word is protect, which has the flavor of conservation (Pukui and Elbert 1986: 233–234).

KEKELA, KONOHIKI

As was the custom of *aliʻi* with widespread estates, *konohiki* were appointed to care for the resources found in outlying *ahupuaʻa* and ensure that the activities of the *makaʻāinana* ran smoothly. Kekela, a close relative of Pākī was appointed by him as *konohiki* of Hāʻena.

E. Kekela was a sister of Pākī's mother. Kekela was originally married to a half brother of Kamehameha I. After her husband's death she was given by Kamehameha I to Kamaholelani as part of the negotiations that brought Kauaʻi into the federation of islands forged by Kamehameha I and his Hawaiʻi island *aliʻi*. In 1810, she settled with Kamaholelani (sometimes referred to as a cousin or son of Kaumualiʻi) on Kauaʻi in the *ahupuaʻa* of Lumahaʻi, a few miles east of Hāʻena (Kamakau 1992: 195). Kamaholelani died in 1820; Kekela remained in Lumahaʻi until 1824, when she returned to Oʻahu, and either forfeited or was dispossessed of Lumahaʻi as a result of the civil strife occurring during the Kauaʻi "Rebellion" of 1824. Although we do not have many details about this war, we know that it caused an enormous upheaval on Kauaʻi for both *aliʻi* and *makaʻāinana*. In the aftermath of this conflict, even those Kauaʻi *aliʻi* loyal to the Kamehameha government were divested of their *ahupuaʻa*. A short excursion into this little known part of Hawaiian history will help explain who got what on Kauaʻi in the Mahele of 1848.

The death of Kaumualiʻi, *mōʻī* of Kauaʻi, relatively soon after the death of Kamehameha I created a very unsettled state of affairs regarding land on this northern island. *Aliʻi* from Hawaiʻi and other southern islands, followers of Kamehameha I in his campaign to unite all the islands under a single ruler, had been disappointed by the bloodless, diplomatic agreement between Kamehameha I and Kaumualiʻi. In that agreement, Kamehameha refused the lands offered to him by Kaumualiʻi. Kamehameha allowed Kaumualiʻi and his Kauaʻi *aliʻi* to retain responsibility for governing the lands of Kaua'i as long as Kaua'i ali'i recognized Kamehameha as paramount ali'i, or mō'ī. This, however, was contrary to traditional custom, by which the victors of conflicts between ali'i in Hawaiian society divided up the lands of those on the losing side. These are the words of Kamehameha to Kaumuali'i:

> "This is my gift at our meeting, the land of Kauai, its chiefs, its men great and small, from mountain to sea, all above and below, and myself to be yours." Kamehameha said, "I shall not accept your land, not the least portion of your domain. Return and rule over it. But if our young chief [Liholiho, son of Kamehameha] makes you a visit, be pleased to receive him."
> Kamakau 1961: 196

Therefore, there would be no kālai 'āina (carving of the land), the traditional awarding of lands to allies of victorious ali'i in the aftermath of war. Hawai'i island ali'i, and those fighting men of Kamehameha I who had not yet been awarded lands, were disgruntled, but could do nothing about it. Years later, many Kaua'i ali'i also expected a kālai 'āina after the death of Kaumuali'i, but he froze the lands by pronouncing on his deathbed "Let the lands be as they are, those chiefs who have lands to hold them, those who have not to have none" (Kamakau 1961: 265).

When Kaumuali'i died, many Kaua'i ali'i and maka'āinana expected a son of Kaumuali'i, George Humehume, to become mō'ī of Kaua'i. But Kaumuali'i had been taken as husband/hostage by the widow of Kamehameha I, Ka'ahumanu, and had died on O'ahu in the presence of the family and allies of Kamehameha. His last wish concerning who would take his place, therefore, was interpreted by a council of ali'i to mean that his nephew, Kahalaia, would be governor of Kaua'i. Kahalaia established himself at Fort Hipo in Waimea, in the Kona district of Kaua'i. Firearms and soldiers stationed there represented the Kamehameha dynasty. After Kaumuali'i died, some Kaua'i ali'i led by Humehume and their supporters stormed the fort with only wooden spears and digging sticks. They were repulsed by the armed soldiers.

News of the uprising brought recruits from O'ahu aboard more than ten ships descending upon Kaua'i with firearms, slaughtering the Kaua'i contingent. After the war of 1824, all Kaua'i ali'i, even those loyal to Kamehameha, were dispossessed of their lands. Kamakau raises some questions about these events echoed by some Kauaians even today (personal communication, Joe Manini 1999).

> After the battle, the chiefs came together and Ka-lani-moku redistributed the lands of Kauai. Was this right? What about Kamehameha's agreement with Ka-umu-ali'i? What about Liholiho's promise? What about the last will of Ka-umu-ali'i at Pakaka? Some Kauai chiefs were on Maui attending the

burial of their dead ruler [he was buried in Lahaina], some fought loyally
against the rebels; yet their lands were seized with the others. The last will
of Ka-umu-ali'i, who had the real title *to the lands, was not respected.*
Kamakau 1961: 268, emphasis added

KEKELA'S CLAIM AND AWARD

The war of 1824 might explain why Kekela lost her position as *konohiki* of Lumaha'i under Konia, but she came back to Kaua'i appointed by Pākī as *konohiki* of
Hā'ena. It is here we find her in the historic record contained in early land documents concerning Hā'ena.

Established as *konohiki* in 1837, Kekela registered at the time of the Kuleana Act
of 1850 a claim as *konohiki* having authority over *kō'ele*. *Kō'ele* were *lo'i* (pond fields
for growing taro) traditionally cared for and cultivated by the *maka'āinana* but
whose produce was reserved for the *ali'i* of the *ahupua'a*. Kekela is one of several
female *konohiki* claiming and being awarded land. Though women were rarely
awarded land, in Hā'ena a few widows and female heirs of longtime residents did
apply for land. Perhaps Kekela's presence as *konohiki* of Hā'ena encouraged a
higher than usual number of women to file their claims. Here is Kekela's claim:

> *Hear ye, ye Commissioners to Quiet Land Titles living at Hale Kauwila,*
> *Honolulu, Oahu, greetings: I, E. Kekela, a woman Konohiki, a Hawaiian*
> *subject, having authority over the ko'eles in the Ahupua'a of Haena,*
> *island of Kauai hereby tell of the number of ko'eles to which there is a*
> *right from formerly until this 31 day of January 1848. It is not possible*
> *for me to tell their dimensions because they are so numerous. I hereby*
> *give their names: Paki, Kahookumaka, Oahu, Kapalaa, there are two;*
> *Akole and Haleahuine, Mailiili, Peekauai, Kalaole and Kailiili, Koi,*
> *Kanaele, Keokea. KEKELA, Haena, Kauai, 31 January 1848.*

Witnesses verify her claims, describing the lands in relation to other lands and
identifying the natural features surrounding them. Though she claimed five
parcels—one in Wai'oli and four in Hā'ena—she was awarded only four parcels
in L.C.A. 7947 and 5477 comprising a house lot in Hā'ena, two *loko kalo* (taro
ponds) in Hā'ena, and a house lot in Wai'oli ahupua'a, several miles from Hā'ena
but still in Halele'a district.

Out of the twenty-one Land Commission Awards granted in Hā'ena, fourteen
awards were for single parcels of land. In many other areas of Kaua'i, claimants
generally received two parcels—a house lot and a parcel of land for cultivating
taro. Only five of the Hā'ena awards contained two parcels; two claimants were
awarded three parcels. It seems that in some cases, house sites were located close
enough to the *lo'i* that it was more practical to include both in one parcel of land.

In sharp contrast to the process of the Mahele, whereby *ali'i* were able to separate out their lands by name alone, *maka'āinana* were held to a more rigorous standard. In order to make successful claims, *maka'āinana* had to produce two witnesses verifying the claim was legitimate and that the claimants had been living on the lands prior to 1839. They also had to hire a surveyor to perform and submit a Western-style survey (metes and bounds) of the property and finally pay a fee in order to receive an award.

Testimony from witnesses brought by claimants was collected in both languages, English (Foreign Testimony) and Hawaiian (Native Testimony). Surprisingly, at least twenty-four of the witnesses from Hā'ena, who were purportedly residents of the area, did not submit claims for land when given the opportunity under the Kuleana Act. This raises certain questions. Who were these people brought as witnesses? Why didn't they apply for land? Were they family members who lived on the land but were not heads of households, and therefore either felt they did not qualify or did not think it was necessary to submit claims? The extensive complex of stone walls delineating the traditionally cultivated lands

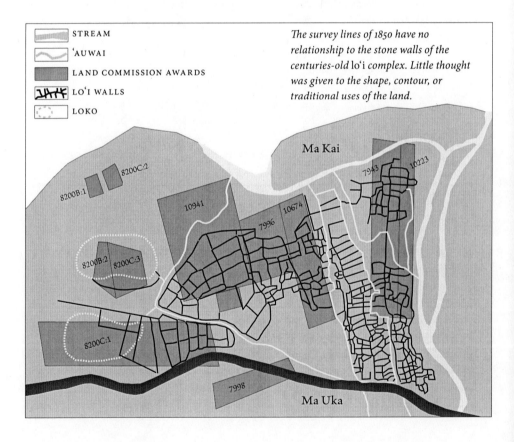

The survey lines of 1850 have no relationship to the stone walls of the centuries-old lo'i complex. Little thought was given to the shape, contour, or traditional uses of the land.

still stands in Hāʻena. When one compares the surveyed boundaries of the lands awarded in 1850 to the available cultivatable land in the area, it is clear that many acres of *loʻi* were not claimed or awarded. In hindsight, it seems as if there was more than enough *ʻāina* for more individuals to have registered and received claims.

Some of those who did not claim land acted as witnesses for those who did seem to have been family members. Testimony (Foreign Testimony vol. 12, 151–152) for L.C.A. 9179 records that the claimant, Kaukapawa, had two sons, Kumukamaliʻi and Pukoula, who cultivated a part of his *loʻi*. Old enough to cultivate the land, they apparently were not interested or did not think it necessary to claim land of their own. Does this mean that those who did not submit claims felt their interests in Hāʻena *ʻāina* were still undivided and remained in the *ahupuaʻa* to be claimed at a later date? This question continues to be raised by scholars of Hawaiian history and activists for indigenous Hawaiian rights.

Once the *kuleana* were awarded and the original awardee passed away, families were forced to divide up what was already a tiny portion of land granted by the original award. In many cases, within a single generation, the awarded lands proved insufficient to allow children of the original awardees to survive on the land.

In traditional times, whether within the *ahupuaʻa* of one's birth or in another of one's choice, a person only needed to demonstrate the ability to *mālama* (care for) the *ʻāina* in order to receive land for a living space and access to land for production. The ability to work with other people to make the land productive made long-term survival and prosperity possible. Under the new land use regime, succeeding generations of aboriginal people had to limit their endeavors to the land awarded or, if more land was necessary, they would have to buy it from another entity, either private or governmental. There is evidence to support the observation that some did not claim land because they felt it was not necessary. They believed life would go on as it had for the past two thousand years. When it became necessary to cultivate more land, they would do so by working it out in the traditional method of investing labor and time. As stated earlier, there is evidence also that some did not submit claims because they did not want to offend *aliʻi* and also that certain unscrupulous *aliʻi* actually intimidated *makaʻāinana* who indicated interest in claiming land under the new regime instituted by the Mahele and Kuleana Act.

From this point in history on, *ahupuaʻa* inhabitants not awarded a *kuleana* would have to purchase or rent the means to produce their livelihood, most often compelling them to enter the cash market economy. Many abandoned the land and moved to port towns. Even those awarded *kuleana* would have to "rent" the land from the government by paying real estate taxes in cash in perpetuity. Failure to pay these taxes meant forfeiting the land. The *makaʻāinana* had no choice: they were forced to enter the cash economy. Bringing the cultivated fruits of the land and sea and the work of their hands and offering them to Lono in Makahiki would no longer guarantee their ability to live upon the lands. Currency would now be the only acceptable form of balancing out responsibilities to society and government.

Taxation not only coerced people into earning cash, it undermined the traditional relationships *ali'i* and *maka'āinana* had enjoyed over centuries. Traditional checks and balances in the *ahupua'a* serving to curb abuses of power and promote relatively egalitarian relationships between *ali'i* and *maka'āinana* were displaced by foreign concepts of law necessitating judges, lawyers, and legal paraphernalia. The imposed market economy and Euro-American systems of jurisprudence/land tenure in which the Native people were now enmeshed would unravel and erode traditional familial relationships they enjoyed with the land, its creatures, and each other.

MAKA'ĀINANA AWARDS

In order to receive an award of land under the Kuleana Act, *maka'āinana* were required to submit a written claim and have two witnesses verify their claim. Each claimant needed to identify how he or she came to live on the land claimed. According to the testimony recorded at the time, some of the lands awarded to *maka'āinana* had been held since ancient times. While Kaumuali'i is mentioned as grantor of the land to six claimants in Hā'ena, other claimants simply said the land had been given to them by *konohiki* from ancient times without mentioning a specific name. Several *konohiki* names—Kalaniulumoku, Kamoku'ohai, Kaikioewa, and Kamo'opohaku—are mentioned in the testimony. Of course, Kekela, as the one holding the position during this critical time in the history of Hā'ena, played an important role in granting land to *maka'āinana*.

Four claimants identify Kekela as the person who gave them their land. For six others who submitted claims for land in Hā'ena to the Land Commission, she is the sole witness. Since the Land Commission required two witnesses to validate most claims, it is an indication of Kekela's status as *konohiki,* and possibly as *ali'i,* that the Land Commission honored these claims solely on her testimony. The record does however contain a difference of opinion regarding L.C.A. 8200-B for Nanahu:

> *This land had been from Kaumualii to the grandparents, then to his parents and from them it went to his older brother and finally to Nanahu himself. The land is more secured at this time but during the time of Kekela, the new Konohiki disputed the claim. Nanahu received this land from his brother at the time Kaikioewa died in 1839. Mokuohai came to Haena in 1840, he asked Nanahu for a house lot and after he had built his house, he asked Nanahu for farm land that he might have food. Nanahu also let him have a part of the pond. Nanahu asked Mokuohai to return*

the land to him after his harvest but Kekela is now giving this land out-right to Mokuohai. Native Testimony vol. 12, 160–162

Though the testimony for L.C.A. 8200-C for Mokuohai confirms his award, it actually went to his grandchild and heir, Kaenaku. L.C.A. 7943 (Keahiahi) intimates that the *konohiki* had intervened for a time in the piece of land that Keahiahi would claim and eventually be awarded:

> *These lands were given by the Konohiki to the father of Claimant in the reign of Kaumualii by whom they were held in peace till his death about 1848. The Konohiki took them for a short time when they were given to Claimant who has held them in peaceable possession till this time.* Foreign Testimony vol. 12, 92–93

Several other awards went to individuals other than the claimants, including children, widows, and husbands of widows who had been heirs. How the original claimants died is often uncertain. Did they die of old age, or were they victims of the diseases from elsewhere that annihilated the Hawaiian population beginning in the time of Captain Cook? Much has been written regarding the tremendous population decline as a result of the diseases (Stannard 1989; Kuykendall 1938; Schmitt 1968). The small number of claims filed for Hāʻena in the mid-1800s stands in stark contrast to the extensive network of stone walls delineating many acres of *loʻi* found in Hāʻena but not claimed by anyone. Unclaimed and out of production today, they are evidence of a much larger population on the land in pre-European times:

> *L.C.A. 7945 Kekula*
> *These lands were given by the Konohiki in about 1839 to the husband of Kekula. He has died & the widow held the lands till she married again. She is now dead & the lands are held by her last husband Makumahu.* Foreign Testimony vol. 12, 87–88

> *L.C.A. 7946 Kanuiopu (w)*
> *These lands were given by the Konohiki previous to 1829 to Claimant's husband. He has died & the lands were held by the widow till she married again. Her present husband has held them in undisturbed possession till this time.* Foreign Testimony vol. 12, 87

> *L.C.A. 10223 Moe*
> *Moe died in 1850, his wife now has the land, no disputes.* Native Testimony vol. 12, 100

L.C.A. 10674 Pea
I came to Haena in 1839 & Pea (10674) was there in possession of these
lands. He had held them from the days of Kamualii. No one disputed his
claim up to his death in 1849. His widow now holds them in peaceable
possession. Foreign Testimony vol. 12, 94

L.C.A. 10940 Uiha
These lands have been held by Uiha & his parents from the days of
Kaumualii. Claimant's mother died in 1841 when the lands were in
the quiet possession & no one has disputed the claim till now.
Foreign Testimony vol. 12, 151

Another curiosity found in the land documents is that three claimants actually lived on the house lot of Kekela. Possibly retainers of the *ali'i,* they perhaps lived in a *kauhale,* a collection of separate structures forming many traditional households, and in the case of *ali'i,* often included structures housing their retainers.

L.C.A. 7967 Keahiaka
Claimant has a house in Kekela's yard where he has lived since his
residence at Haena. Foreign Testimony vol. 12, 86

L.C.A. 7996 Kanehakili
Claimant has a house in the lot of Kekela where he has resided since 1839.
Foreign Testimony vol. 12, 88

L.C.A. 10562 Opu
(Kekela sworn says . . .) I gave the moo Kanakapili & the yard that is
fenced in 1839. The Loko Keaualoko was then in possession of Opu &
had been for some Years. These lands have all been held in peaceable
possession till now. Opu has a house in my yard which I recognize as
a claim for a house lot. Foreign Testimony vol. 12:, 89–90

From a Native perspective, the spirit of the Mahele and the Kuleana Act meant that while the *maka'āinana* had primary responsibility and authority over the lands awarded them, the *konohiki* and the *ali'i* still held primary authority and responsibility over the remaining lands within the *ahupua'a. Maka'āinana,* however, retained the rights of access to resources within the *ahupua'a,* including but not limited to access, water, fire, and gathering, ensuring their ability to provide themselves with the means of subsistence, health, and a measure of prosperity. In addition, the question of what happened to the interests held by those who did not submit claims still remains somewhat controversial. The process of law, often swayed by Euro-American perspectives and views, had very different ideas about the meaning of rights and the relationship of people to the land, as history has shown.

Given how Hawaiian societal relationships evolved historically, it is clear that when the new system of law interpreted these rights, it was often blind to what people had been doing from time immemorial in the islands, giving priority to Euro-American perspectives—especially to those with access to economic and political power. It would be through interpretations and decisions about rights that the newly formed, foreign-influenced Hawaiian government and the courts the American system imposed upon Hawai'i after it was annexed as an American territory in 1898 that many *maka'āinana* would be driven off their lands (Lam 1985: 115–118).

By drawing artificial boundaries, the division of the land under the Mahele and Kuleana Act began a process that restricted the ability of *maka'āinana* to access and sustain themselves through resources within the *ahupua'a*. *Maka-'āinana* were even more constrained when ownership of *ahupua'a* came into the hands of foreigners, which happened in a large majority of cases. In Hā'ena, the situation evolved in a slightly different way than happened elsewhere. Here, Native Hawaiians, by pooling their resources, were successful in acquiring ownership and most of the control over land considerably longer than in other areas. This contributed greatly toward their ability to exercise traditional customs and practices, at least until the 1960s. The chapters that follow explain in more detail what actually transpired. In many parts of Hawai'i, when carried to "letter of the law" extremes and enforced by a legal system slanted increasingly toward Euro-American antecedents, the system of land boundaries made it progressively more difficult, sometimes impossible, for *maka'āinana* to get from their *pā hale* (house lots, where they carried on their domestic activities) to their *lo'i kalo* (irrigated terraces where they cultivated the staff of life, *kalo*), and in some cases to the fishing grounds and mountain areas, without resorting to litigation.

The *mō'ī, ali'i,* and government were recipients of awards containing large portions of or, in many cases, entire *ahupua'a*. Some of these lands located far from Honolulu, like Hā'ena, were often first to be sold, especially those with little potential for sugar planting or grazing cattle (Stauffer 1989: 145). Opinions vary on why *ali'i* lands were alienated so quickly after the Mahele. Ironically, the traditional responsibility of *ali'i* to support their retainers, often family members, seems to have been a contributing factor. Many *ali'i,* when they became aware they were land-rich but cash-poor, still felt responsible for the support of these relatives and retainers. Therefore, their overhead was burdensome. The new system of laws, having severed the traditional reciprocal relationships connecting *maka'āinana* and *ali'i* that had kept both in a state of relative prosperity in traditional times, left these *ali'i* experiencing difficulty in maintaining the lifestyle to which they were accustomed. *Ali'i* who still felt responsible for supporting their retainers often found they had to sell land or risk it to secure loans.

New laws, survey lines, ideas of private property, and demands of the taxation system virtually eliminated the traditional labor exchange relationships binding *maka'āinana* and *ali'i* together. After the Mahele, *ali'i* might have owned large areas of land, but they had no one to work the land, to make it productive. *Maka'āinana* had to earn cash in the new market economy to pay the taxes required by government and to buy goods from foreigners, like cloth for clothes now required by the new Christian morality. *Maka'āinana,* now investing their time and energy earning enough cash to keep themselves solvent, were no longer bound by mutual affection and reciprocal responsibilities to *ali'i,* most especially to those absentee *ali'i* now ensconced in port towns. Selling the lands awarded them in the Mahele often became the option chosen by *ali'i* wishing to enjoy status in the new society.

CASH

Many *maka'āinana,* especially those not granted land, also left their *ahupua'a* in post-Mahele times. Often they settled in towns or near seaports where cash, almost entirely derived from foreign sources, was more available. The need to access sources of cash was a major reason people left the *ahupua'a.* They could no longer pay their debts and taxes with products of subsistence life ways or satisfy their obligations to society through contributions of shared labor, as they had in the traditional system (Merry 2000: 98–99).

Although many *ahupua'a* were sold to *haole* (foreigners), a significant number (Watson 1932: 9) were sold to groups of *maka'āinana* who organized *hui kū'ai 'āina* (cooperatives to buy land) as a means to raise the cash necessary to purchase lands being offered for sale. In some cases, *ali'i* owners of *ahupua'a* offered the first chance to buy these lands to the *maka'āinana* residents. Not particularly suited for commercial use or sugar cultivation, Hā'ena probably seemed like the end of the world to those who dwelt in the burgeoning new city of Honolulu, where Pākī, his daughter Pauahi, and his son-in-law Charles Reed Bishop lived.

Having become used to the more urbane Western lifestyle and often because the source of their livelihood was in the new urban environment, many *ali'i* no longer regularly traveled to personally visit their lands outside of the new mainstream as they had traditionally done. In pre-Euro-American times, *ali'i* traveled often to outlying *ahupua'a,* residing there for long periods of time and staying in direct contact with the lands and their *maka'āinana.* Since the Mahele severed the traditional link between *ali'i* and *maka'āinana* making it possible for *ali'i* to call out large workforces, they no longer had access to this important element that once balanced societal relationships and made for what one writer has called "subsistence prosperity." Without the cooperation of *maka'āinana,* most remaining *ahupua'a* land suitable for agriculture could not produce cash crops without a considerable personal investment of labor and/or capital by the *ali'i*. The sale or mortgage of land to produce cash for the *ali'i* and their retainers was often a quick solution. What happened in Hā'ena followed this general pattern. An *'ōlelo no'eau* of those times described how some of the people felt about the *ali'i* divesting themselves of the lands and their accompanying responsibility to the people.

> *'O ke ali'i lilo i ka le'ale'a a mālama 'ole i ke kanaka me kapu akua,*
> *'a'ole ia he ali'i e ku ai i ka moku.*

> *The ali'i who is taken with pleasure seeking and cares not for the*
> *welfare of the people or the observation of the kapu of the akua,*
> *is not the chief who will become a leader.*
> Pukui 1983: 267–268

HUI KŪ'AI 'ĀINA

About 2,500 acres of Hā'ena had been granted to Abner Pākī, which he kept until his death in 1855. Pauahi, his daughter, inherited Hā'ena *ahupua'a;* her husband, Charles Reed Bishop, was the first successful banker in Hawai'i. A very powerful figure during this period, he was well versed in the skills necessary in the new system of capital and property instituted by the Mahele. In 1866, W. H. Pease, a surveyor of the period (later identified by some as being the most inaccurate surveyor of the time), bought Hā'ena for $1,200 from the Bishops (Bureau of Conveyances, Liber 10, 144). In 1872, the *ahupua'a* was then conveyed by deed from the administrators of Pease's estate (who apparently had passed away) to William Kinney of Hanalei, Kaua'i, who successfully bid $1,200 at the estate auction (Bureau of Conveyances, Liber 35, 108). In January 1875, Kinney, who in the interim had moved from Kaua'i and was living in Onomea, Hawai'i island, conveyed/covenanted with Kenoi D. Kaukaha and thirty-seven others known collectively as the Hui Kū'ai 'Āina o Hā'ena, the "organization to purchase land in Hā'ena." The land from that point on was owned and held in common by this group for close to a hundred years (Bureau of Conveyances, Liber 52, 100–101).

The *hui* was one of many associations formed by *maka'āinana* throughout the islands to buy land in post-Mahele/Kuleana Act times. Although not well known, the story of this movement gives voice to a short-lived counteroffensive against the ongoing alienation of land and dispossession brought on by the new regime of private property and real estate. Although the Kuleana Act entitled subsistence gathering, access, and water use rights to *maka'āinana* awardees, in many cases, this was not enough to guarantee the means of survival provided by their former, cooperative practices: customary rights to the resources of the *ahupua'a* and the traditional system of reciprocal responsibility. Although it did not occur in Hā'ena, the increasingly Western-oriented government acquired large portions of the *ahupua'a* lands in Hawai'i. In the aftermath of the Mahele and Kuleana Act, the government sold much of the land it had acquired through deeds called Royal Patent Grants. Although numbers of Hawaiians acquired lands in this way, *haole* (foreigners), having capital, were able to afford most of the larger parcels. The government subdivided some of their acquired lands into small strips, and sold it for fifty cents an acre to *maka'āinana*, including families dispossessed by the Mahele, those who had not gotten enough land, and those who had come of age after the Land Commission stopped accepting claims (Fornander 1999). However, the great majority of acreage, at least in Halele'a, went to *haole*.

MAKA'ĀINANA LETTERS

Letters from *maka'āinana* to the Interior Department contain the voices of the dispossessed, and provide a looking glass into the kinds of hardships *maka-'āinana* faced as they adjusted to the new property regime. The following letter by *maka'āinana* in Wai'oli, an *ahupua'a* several miles from Hā'ena, shows how lost and confused *maka'āinana* were feeling as a result of the changes turning their world upside down. They compare themselves to the *kōlea* (plover), a bird migrating from Alaska to Hawai'i every year, disappearing in spring when it returns to its breeding grounds in the far north having fattened itself on the bounty of the islands during the winter.

> *Love to you with peace.*
>
> *We humbly make petition to you with love. We wish to lease Waioli by the year, at $200. Per annum, so that our animals and children will be provided, and we can live in comfort. According to what God has given equally unto all the people and the chiefs of this Government. We are just like plovers which live at the points along the seashore, without being settled, and if you consent, your subjects will be happy, and if it is transferred to the foreigners, what a pity, your subjects will be wanderers. The same as the goats in the forests, if you refuse to lease, the mountains will be the place where we will be, the trees will be our home with the firewood. You think of what has been received for the years gone by, we believe that it very proper (pono loa) that you consent. If your mind be the same as God's we will not oppose you and what belongs to the chiefs, it is very proper that the ability to live here become ours, your obedient subjects, in order that we become the children of this land of Waioli (i lilo makou he poe kamaaina no keia aina o Waioli).*
>
> *Na makou me ke aloha, kou mau makaainana.*
> *(From us with love, your makaainana)*
>
> Letter to Keoni Ana, Department of the Interior Land Files, from "your subjects at Wai'oli" [letter not signed], January 6, 1852.

Another 1852 letter to Keoni Ana reveals that *maka'āinana* were not only distressed at being driven away from their lands, but were encountering problems because of the changing land uses the new landholding class was putting into practice. Homes of the *maka'āinana* were made of grass. Barbed or any other kind of wire was practically nonexistent at the time, let alone affordable to these people.

> *We complain to you of our trouble, this is the first trouble, our houses*
> *are destroyed by the cattle, the second trouble is about our gardens, our*
> *crops are trampled on by the cattle, the third, our being driven away, but*
> *our greatest distress is that there is no more good places (kahi pono ole)*
> *of this land remaining, so that we might buy some acres for us.*
> Letter to Keoni Ana, Department of Interior Land File, January 5, 1852

It would be a mistake to think that because the Mahele was framed almost entirely in Hawaiian words, the theory underlying it and its outcomes were the results of Native Hawaiian thinking. The Mahele was largely instigated and carried out by *haole* (foreigners); the way *kuleana* and *ahupua'a* were granted in the Mahele did not reflect the traditional relationships and interests of the *ali'i* and the *maka'āinana*. And although this chapter has been about what took place over a century and a half ago, the process of alienating Hawaiians from the land continues.

Nancy: Before time was all good, but not now. Now the haole *come in they not like before* haole. *The Wichman, the Isenberg, the Brown, the one that owned that lot before, down Hā'ena, the one off the road. Married Hawaiian! We call her Aunty Rose.*

That's how Hawaiians had all their land, cause get lot of taro, Kelau, lot of taro, everything. Had lot of Hawaiians, lots of Hawaiians! But when they took the land away uh you know the State or whatever, the land from my uncle and, condemn the place they said that they was going make roads and park or something. But look they only talk and take the land away from the Hawaiians plus what they give him?

Wainiha, Haalelea. Kauai Aug 29 1881

I keia la 29 o Augate A.D. 1881,
ua noi mai ka poe no lakou na apana
aina malalo iho i na Luna o ka aina
e hookaawalea keia mau wahi a
pau loa malalo iho nei no lakou, o
nolaila, o makou o na Luna i kohoia
no ka hookaawale ana, ke hoike nei
ua hookaawale loa ia aku ia mau
apana aina a pau loa, no lakou, a no
ko lakou mau Hooilina, na Luna
Hooponopono Waiwai, a me ko lakou
mau Hope a pau loa e like me ke
Kanawai; no ka manawa pau ole,
ma o ko lakou mau Kuleana la
iloko o ka "Hui Kuai Aina o Wainiha. A penei na palena o na mau
apana aina ka.

I No D. Nienihiwa. malofetokofede

E hoomaka ana ma ke kihi Ko. Ak.
o ko James J. Robinson, a holo ana penei,
S 51° W 1.34 Kaul. ma ko J.J. Robinson
S 43° W 4.35   "   "   "
S 47½° W 2.83   "   " Keikemui
N 14½° W 5.33   "   " Kahawai
N 24° E 5.36   "   "   "
N 42½ E 15.80   "   "   "
S 48° E 2.39   "   "   "
S 40¾ W 3.76   "   " Makauai
S 54¼° W 4.43   "   "   "
S 8½° W 2.18   "   " Kilii & Punawawa
S 2° W 1.66   "   "   "
S 30° W 4.50   "   "   "
a hiki i kahi i hoomakai.
8 Eka, 3 R. 11½ Peka more or less.
Koe ke Kuleana o Kamaka.

Page from the original handwritten by-laws of Hui Kūʻai ʻĀina o Wainiha.
Hawaiʻi State Archives.

CHAPTER FIVE

HUI KŪʻAI ʻĀINA O HĀʻENA

 HUI KŪʻAI ʻĀINA O HĀʻENA (Hāʻena Cooperative/
Company to Purchase Land) was only one of many *hui* (organizations, gatherings together of people) formed by the people
to buy land in the aftermath of the Mahele and Kuleana Act.
These *hui* came into existence in large part because *makaʻāinana* recognized that lands provided for them by the Mahele and Kuleana Act
were inadequate for continued survival. The manner in which they organized
themselves, as indicated by the bylaws they drafted to guide the activities of their
organizations, also suggests they wanted to retain some features of the traditional
life ways of the ancestors. These *hui* were described and categorized by courts
of law as "unincorporated voluntary associations."

Makaʻāinana who successfully organized themselves in these *hui* raised
capital, seizing opportunities to purchase or lease parts of *ahupuaʻa* not awarded
them. *Hui* documents contain examples of strategies aboriginal Hawaiian people
adopted to enable living in the time-honored ways of their ancestors while at the
same time engaging the more recently arrived market economy and new forms
of governance. They did this through what they felt were legal and peaceful
means. Though these *hui* were common in Hawaiʻi until the 1920s, rules of law
were interpreted to suit newer voices on the land. What follows is a preamble
taken from a handwritten book housed in the State Archives documenting the
bylaws for the organization of the Wainiha Hui. It is the only original book
of *hui* bylaws in existence for this part of Kauaʻi.

> *Kumukanawai o ka Hui Kuai Aina o Wainiha* A.D. 1877.
>
> *Pauku 1. Ua Hui kekahi poe Kanaka Hawaii Ponoi e kuai i kekahi aina
> i kapa ia o Wainiha no na dala elima Tausani elima haneri ($5,500.)
> Ua hoomaka ia keia kuai ana i Ianuali* A.D. 1869.
>
> (*Paragraph 1. Certain Native Hawaiians have organized themselves to
> purchase the land known as Wainiha for sum of five thousand, five hun-
> dred dollars. The payments have commenced in January of 1869.*)

Constitution of the Association of Wainiha to Buy Land, A.D. 1877

The attempts of Native *hui* to keep to their traditional life ways were generally thwarted by a legal system whose balance was shifting more and more toward Western ideas of exclusivity. This was especially true after 1898, as rising numbers of foreigners took up residence in the islands—increasingly so, after the independence of the Hawaiian nation was dispensed with and the little island nation was absorbed as a territory of the United States. One Supreme Court case (*Smythe v. Takara,* 26 Haw 69, 1921, more commonly known as Maalo) triggered legislation (Partition Act 1923) calling for the partition of the *hui* (Watson 1932: 16). The outcome of these suits for partition was the application of a rule of law compelling *hui* to divide the land, fragmenting forever the communally based system that had served the Hawaiian people so well.

In Hā'ena, the *ahupua'a* stayed intact for longer than most *hui* lands, continuing to be held in common by the heirs, agents, and successors of the original *hui* well into the 1960s. The suit for partition finally fragmenting the *ahupua'a* was not initiated until 1955. Two wealthy *haole,* having purchased shares from family members and heirs of individuals who had been part of the original *hui,* brought the suit before the courts. This initiation of partition suits dealing with *hui* lands by wealthy individuals or entities who had purchased shares in *hui* was a frequent occurrence in the years following the annexation of Hawai'i as a U.S. territory.

An examination of records documenting conveyances of property on the island of Kaua'i occurring in the decades following annexation reveals that scions of missionary and early *haole* entrepreneurial families acquired large amounts of *kuleana* land (grant land) as well as shares in *hui* land. This was due, in large part, to their greater access to resources of cash. More often than not, there were water rights attached to these lands that could be sold separately from the land itself. During this time, influential *haole,* many who had been born and raised in the islands, became officers of the *hui* governing bodies due to their high political and economic status in island society. This was so in Hā'ena.

Formed at the time when *maka'āinana* felt constrained by foreign-inspired legalities, early *hui* suffered from their members' limited experience with the new legal and economic system, especially the workings of capitalism. In fact, as indicated in their bylaws, *hui* generally seemed committed to customary and traditional practices. In many cases, members of the original *hui* were born before the Mahele, and from the records they left behind, seem to have been attempting to reassert some of the life ways of pre-Euro-American times by articulating them in the bylaws of their organizations. A fundamental precept for *hui* was sharing, collectively, a large tract of land. The opportunity offered by *hui* ownership of *ahupua'a* was far more adaptable to Hawaiian needs, customary uses, and traditional practices than Euro-American-inspired ideas of individual ownership in small disconnected parcels (Watson 1932: 9).

ORIGINAL SHAREHOLDERS OF THE HĀʻENA HUI

As mentioned earlier, in January 1875, William Kinney, who at the time owned
Hāʻena, but in the interim had moved from Kauaʻi to take up residence in Ono-
mea, Hawaiʻi island, sold it to the thirty-eight original shareholders of the Hui
Kūʻai ʻĀina o Hāʻena. All original members of the Hui were Native Hawaiians.
However, by the time the lawsuit for partition was filed in 1955, the makeup of
the Hui had changed considerably. All shares adjudicated in the partition of the
Hāʻena lands, however, were derived from the original shareholders in the Hui.
Some shares had been passed down and continued to be held by families. Often,
in Hawaiian families, shares were fragmented into very small percentages. Each
original owner's share was divided among his heirs. In a number of cases, each
of the children's fractional shares was further divided among the succeeding
generation. Each generation further fragmented the original share. Some shares
were sold or conveyed by other means. Those with access to capital, many who
were wealthy *haole,* were often the beneficiaries of these sales. In some cases,
these purchases were entire shares from original shareholders.

The following individuals were the original members of the Hui Kūʻai ʻĀina
o Hāʻena listed in order of their share numbers:

1. Kaukaha	14. Apolo	27. Paamaui
2. Kaahukoo	15. Kainalu	28. Makahuki
3. Kahilikolo	16. Hale	29. Nakaloilani
4. Napuamauu	17. Kuehuehu	30. Uo
5. Huakahi	18. Naai	31. Pili
6. Kale Wahine	19. Aumona	32. Upai
7. Paamaui	20. Kapiiohi	33. Keoki
8. J. W. Lota	21. Piilani	34. Kealohi
9. Henrietta	22. Enoka	35. Kalue
10. Emalia Hale	23. Kaui	36. Keliihune
11. Z. Seta	24. Beni	37. Nihoa
12. Kahea	25. Kauka	38. Pili
13. Paahao	26. Pueo	

In 1954, John W. Gregg and Paul Rice sued the heirs of Hannah K. Ahi et al.
in the fifth circuit court (Kauaʻi). Gregg was a scion of a wealthy entrepreneur,
a philanthropist, and a resident of Monticello, Illinois. Rice was a descendant
of an early missionary family. Even after the Native population became Christian and the islands were no longer considered a mission field, a goodly number
of missionary families remained. Hawaiʻi became their home.

Descendants of these missionary families were well educated in comparison to the Natives, often as a result of having been sent abroad to schools in New England and other places outside of Hawai'i. In most cases, these children of missionaries did not necessarily follow in the evangelical footsteps of their religious forebears. More often than not, they became entrepreneurs and businessmen. More than a few were able to amass considerable fortunes, in part because of the local connections forged by the original missionaries with their congregations, and in part because of access to considerably more economic resources than most of the aboriginal people had.

In addressing the suit for partitioning, the first task of the court was to identify the shareholders of the Hui and to determine the extent of each of their shares. In Hā'ena, there were three main categories of land: Hui lands (those originally awarded in the Mahele award to Pākī and later purchased from Kinney by the Hui); *kuleana* lands (Land Commission Awards resulting from the Kuleana Act); grants (land granted by the government of the Hawaiian Nation for certain purposes). The *kuleana* and the grant lands (there was only one land grant) were excluded from the process of the partition. According to the documents produced by the lawsuit, the gross area of the whole *ahupua'a* was approximately 1,800 acres. The gross area of the exclusions (L.C.A.s and land grant) was approximately forty-one acres.

The *kuleana* lands had undergone changes in ownership (fragmentation of title within Hawaiian families and sales to both *haole* and *kama'āina* families) similar to those affecting *hui* ownership since the initial awards were made in 1850. Table 1 lists the names of the original awardees of the Land Commission Awards and the names of those who owned these *kuleana* lands when the suit for partition was initiated in 1955.

Many of the owners of Land Commission Award lands in Hā'ena were also shareholders in the Hui lands. Issues of access, gathering, and rights to water for the owners of the *kuleana* parcels needed to be sorted out as the actual work of the partitioning of *hui* lands took place. The original deed from Kinney to the Hui approximated the land to contain an area of 2,500 acres.

LEGALITIES

Initiation of the suit for partition by Gregg and Rice required all shareholders to get legal representation and declare the basis for their ownership. A general order of default against all parties not appearing in person or by counsel or who had not filed answers to the suit was entered. Declarations had to be made and verified by the court for the claims of each shareholder. Some shareholders were minors. A variety of attorneys represented the different parties. These ranged from high-powered attorneys (Howard Moore, Hugh Shearer) from Honolulu on O'ahu to local Japanese American lawyers based on Kaua'i (Jack Mizuha,

Table 1

L.C.A. #	Original Awardee	Owner at Partition
7942	Kuapiko	Uichi Onoue
7943	Keahiahi (ap. 1, 2)	Esther Uo Makaila, Beatrice Kanealii dela Cruz, Joseph Kauwe Kanealii, Raymer K. Kanealii, Robert P. Kanealii, Roger M. Kanealii, Lillian Kanealii Montibon, subject to the curtesy rights of Robert Moewai Kanealii in one-half thereof
7945	Kekulu & Mahu	Madlene Apuna, Florence L. Bannister, Pearl Kapuniai, William Monaha Mason, and George Monaha, subject to the curtesy rights of William Mason Sr.
7946	Kanuiopu	Howard K. Kinney
7949	Kekela (ap. 1, 2, 3)	John W. Gregg
7967	Keahiaka (ap. 1, 2)	Alice Robinson
7998	Haole	County of Kauai
8262	Ohule	William H. Rice, Limited
9140	Kukukaelele	Juliet Wichman
9179	Kaukapawa	George K. Akana, Eugenia Akana and the heirs of Kamealoha
10223	Moa	Benjamin K. Montgomery
10396	Nahialaa	Emma Ouye
10396	Ohule	Emma Ouye
10562	Opu (ap. 1, 2)	Jacob K. Maka, Agnes Thronas, Irene Thronas Strong, Olaf Elia Thronas Jr., Fred Thronas, Samuel Thronas and Bettie Souza, subject to the dower rights of Helen Chun Thronas in one-sixteenth thereof.
10674	Pea	Howard K. Kinney
10941	Naiwi	Kila Pa, Halaki Kelau, Elizabeth Mahuiki Chandler, Marie Mahuiki Inouye, Bernard Mahuiki, Donald Mahuiki, Jeremiah Mahuiki, Lawrence Mahuiki Jr., Ruth Mahuiki, Samson Mahuiki, subject to the dower rights of Rachel Mahuiki in one-fourth thereof.
10965	Wahieloa	Carlos A. W. Long, Elia Long and Leslie M. Pietsch.
7996c	Kanehakili	Paul G. Rice, Kathryn O. Rice
8200b	Nanahu (ap. 1, 2)	Alice Robinson
8200c	Mokuohai (ap. 1, 2 & pt. ii for Kaenaku)	Alice Robinson

Norito Kawakami). Norito Kawakami was appointed as guardian ad litem representing eleven individual minors (all Native Hawaiians) as well as represent as a class of "all additional minors and all incompetent or insane persons and other persons unable by reason of any disability to represent themselves."

Due to the amount of work required to sort out and address all the issues of this complex undertaking, three commissioners were appointed by the courts: Henry C. Wedemeyer (chairman), Yeiso Yamaura, and Nicholas Akana. They were to act under the direction of the court to prepare a plan for the division of the land; to provide for roads and rights of way; to make maps, conduct surveys, and procure appraisements of the values of the property; to investigate and report on the extent of the lands having been occupied by any of the shareholders (also on leases, mortgages, easements, or any liens and encumbrances and amounts involved); to devise drainage and irrigation systems and easements where necessary; and to find and report on the interests of any defendants with interests too small to warrant an apportionment of land.

These commissioners were charged with presenting recommendations to the court concerning the division or allotment of specific parcels of the Hui lands and/or funds of the Hui as to payments, if any, to be made by owners of the Hui lands if the allotments made to them formerly were valued in excess of the value of their interests in the Hui. The commissioners acted as receivers of the court and were to collect all funds and take custody of records, papers, and monies of the Hui as they may have found.

Notifying all who had interests in the *hui* lands would certainly not be an easy task. Families had grown, some had relocated, and many shares had changed hands. A notice of the suit for partition was printed up and posted in three places in Hāʻena; at the end of the government road at Keʻē on the garage door of John Gregg; at the intersection of a side road leading down to the residence of William Chandler; and at the Kauaʻi county park located at Maniniholo. Registered letters were sent to those known to live in other localities. Several of these were sent to young men serving in the armed forces judging by the addresses recorded for them at the time. Sorting out who owned what and from whom each had acquired or inherited shares in the *hui* lands was not without controversy.

The first thing the court did was to collect the records of the Hui. In the first hearing held by the court a large number of the shareholders were present. In the hearing, Charles A. Rice testified that he was the president of the Hui for fifteen years and that the Hui had not been able to obtain a quorum in order to transact any business. As president, he was in possession of all of the Hui documents available at the time. Jacob Maka, the secretary of the Hui, did not have any of the records of the Hui. He also testified to having a one-third interest in the share of Kahea, one of the original shareholders, instead of the one-quarter share that had earlier been recorded. He then recited his genealogy to verify his claim.

Receipt to chief clerk of court for records and the like of Hāʻena Hui indicate that the following were submitted:

1. A passbook with credit balance of $302.17 issued to Charles A. Rice, president of Hui. A cancelled passbook issued to Charles Holokahiki, treasurer. Both passbooks Bank of Hawaiʻi.
2. Two bound minute books of Hui.
3. A certified copy of deed Charles Augustus Brown Estate to John Wyatt Gregg dated February 12, 1945 (Liber 1873, 327–330).
4. A preliminary map of Hāʻena (LCAs and Hui allotments by J. M. Lydgate, October 1915 and retraced March 20, 1949 by M. O.)
5. One box of miscellaneous papers (correspondence, applications for allotments, descriptions etc. relative to Hui).
6. One letter box containing applications for allotments and approvals by board of directors.*

FRAGMENTATION AND ACCUMULATION
In addition to claims submitted by individuals and families, the Territory of Hawaiʻi and the County of Kauaʻi claimed title to certain roadways and easements for public purposes over portions of the Hui lands. There were close to a hundred individuals listed as having shares in the Hui. Table 2 lists the ten largest shareholders in the Hui at the time of the suit for partitioning.

As stated earlier, Native Hawaiian families often had greatly fragmented shares as a result of inheritance and family size. Norito Kawakami, representing individuals who were in that situation, noted that some fractional interests may have been so small that areas of allocable desirable lands would be of little value. Therefore, as long as the families (with the approval of the commissioners) agreed to it, these family members would be able to pool such interests and be awarded a portion of land as tenants in common or otherwise commensurate with the aggregate total interests of the group. Table 3 provides an example of how one original owner's share was fragmented.

The *hui* lands were then classified and placed in several categories as determined by the courts. Value was attached to these lands as the categories dictated. Lands appropriate for growing taro were designated as "wet" lands. Perhaps because *loʻi* lands were entitled to water under the Kuleana Act, shareholders raised motions that these same rights be recognized and written into the partition proceedings. They also agreed that domestic water rights should be attached

---

* Author's note: Attempts to locate the items mentioned in the case files of the fifth circuit court, made in the process of writing this book, were not successful.

Table 2

Owner	Percentage of the Hui
Alice Robinson	17.5501
John Gregg Allerton	12.3651
Paul G. Rice	6.8721
Juliet Wichman	6.7983
County of Kauai	5.2632
Winifred Wilbur Willis	3.5088
Selwyn A. Robinson	2.9034
Dora Jane Cole	2.8288
Dora R. Wallis	2.7367
Rose W. & Wm. J. Chandler	2.4342

to allotments designated as non-*lo'i* lands. Water rights were definitely on many people's minds.

Another issue derived from the fact that certain lands had already been allotted to individuals prior to the suit being brought for partitioning the land. These past allotments were provided for in the original bylaws of the Hui. Hui bylaws established an allotment system whereby each member of the Hui was entitled to select, for his or her exclusive occupancy, certain parcels for homes or agricultural use from the Hui lands. Two-and-a-half acres of *kula* (unirrigated—houselot) land and two-and-a-half acres of "wet" or agricultural land was allotted for each full share owned in the Hui. A lesser amount of land was provided pro rata for fractional shares. All of these transactions had to be approved by the board of directors of the Hui. Because certain allotments of land had already been made to a limited number of shareholders and others had never had an allotment, there was not enough "preferred" land available for those who had not yet been given an allotment. Hence, given that each shareholder was entitled to have an equitable and fair partition of both good as well as the "bad" lands, previous allotments were noted by the court as not to be final.

A counterargument in the process pointed out that those allotments had been in existence since 1877 and that certain shares in the Hui already allotted were purchased for much more than shares without allotments of land. In other words, numerous transactions down through the years had taken place with prices based upon whether the seller did or did not have an allotment. Therefore, a directive by the commissioners that they not be obliged to give full regard to the existing allotments would deny the value of what had actually been paid for the shares having lands already attached to them.

Table 3

Original owner	Shareholder	Percentage of share
# 13 – Hale	Rachel Malia Bickel	0.0556
	Elmer C. Keahi	0.0666
	Joeseph K. Keahi	0.0666
	Norman K. Keahi	0.0666
	Raymond M. Keahi	0.0666
	Winona M. Keahi	0.0666
	Edward Malia	0.0556
	Joseph Malia	0.0556
	William Malia	0.0556
	Caroline Malia Nakamoto	0.0556
	Emma Ouye	0.2779
	Rose Malia Stanley	0.0556
	Pa-u & Maria Waiuli	0.0612

Jack Mizuha, an attorney representing a Native Hawaiian family, moved to amend the order to read that the land should be partitioned in kind as far as practicable; that due regard be given to requests by shareholders who had occupied certain land allotments, especially those upon which improvements had been made in accordance with the rules and the practice of the Hui. All allotments were to be reviewed by the commissioners and subject to redivision in order to effect an equitable partition provided that wherever a home had been established by a shareholder, such home-site together with such an area as was considered reasonable and necessary for the livelihood and use of the home-owner be confirmed to the home owner by the commissioners.

WATER

In partitioning the "wet" lands, the commissioners would determine what amount, if any, of the water of Hāʻena would be given as an appurtenance to any such land.

The County of Kauaʻi had acquired two shares in the *hui*. It had already established a water source and system for drinking water at Mānoa stream and an allotment of land being used as Hāʻena County Park. The county also mentioned that the area at Kēʻē was the only good swimming area in Hāʻena and that in the interest of the public and the growing tourist industry that it should be awarded land at the end of the road there for that purpose.

Another concern was that water rights be awarded to the county from Limahuli stream to support further development of the northern area of the Hui lands. Therefore, the court was asked to award to the county the right to take potable water from Mānoa stream and to keep its easement rights for the water system present at the time; that a million gallons a day be made available to them from Limahuli stream for the northerly lands; that all historical sites and natural attractions be made accessible to the Hui members and the general public; and that the land in Maniniholo, being used as a park, be awarded officially as a park site.

John W. Gregg and Paul G. Rice (plaintiffs) objected to the county claims to water from Limahuli stream. They felt that no water from Limahuli stream or any other source should be made available to the county, other than what was being used under terms of the existing leases at the time between the *hui* and the county. The only exception would be if any such water should also be made available to all other owners of the *hui,* pro rata, according to the ownership of said lands or because of being appurtenant to "wet" or *lo'i* lands. Also, any additional water set aside for the county should be appraised, valued, and form a part of the total valuation of lands or interest to the county because of its pro rata ownership of the Hui. In 1932, the county had leased for twenty-five years all water delivered, drawn, or taken into the pipelines of the county at $5 per million gallons and $25 upon execution of the lease. The proceeds were placed in the custody of Charles A. Rice, who served as president of the Hui at the time. In the end, the county was granted a license to develop water for domestic supply purposes. In addition, portions of the Hui lands were conveyed to the county for a well site, a tank site, easements for access, utility lines, pipes, valves, and a chlorinator.

The Territory of Hawai'i (which after 1959 became the State of Hawai'i) asserted claims to the following: all of the right, title, and interest in and to Grant Forty-one, Apana eight (a school grant) with an appurtenant easement to and from the government road; all right, title, and interest in and to the main government road; an easement for access purposes over and across the existing trail extending from the main government road into the lands of Hanakāpī'ai; and all right, title, and interest of all of those shares in the Hui belonging to those owners who died leaving no heirs. The state (in the 1960s) raised an assertion to land for developing a well. Prior to that time, the county provided residents of Hā'ena with domestic water from surface sources. These surface waters were subject to contamination from animals and other sources, so the development of a well was in the interest of public health. Today, the well is in place and is the source of water serving all of Hā'ena, including vacation rentals and numerous new houses being built there.

STORIED PLACES AND TURF BATTLES

Charles Rice Wichman (one of the shareholders), through his attorney, asked that the court set aside for sale or disposal by gift to the territory all notable places, as more particularly described in the bylaws of the Hui. Other shareholders agreed that these lands be set aside for common use of the owners and the public. These lands included the areas encompassing what are known as the "dry" cave at Maniniholo and the two "wet" caves, Waiakapalae and Waikanaloa, as well as several other sites.

Another issue arising in the partition concerned the efforts of county government to assert its powers over those of the Hui shareholders. The board of supervisors of the County of Kauaʻi attempted to assert their right to preside over the partition of the Hāʻena lands, claiming that laws made by the legislature gave them authority to supervise all subdivisions of land. One argument made, countering the county's assertion, was that the term *subdivision* when applied to partition proceedings was erroneous.

The counterargument did not dispute that presiding over subdivisions was the province of county authorities. However, *hui* partitions fell within the province of the court having jurisdiction where these *hui* were located. It was pointed out that the assumption of jurisdiction by the county was rooted in ordinances established in the City and County of Honolulu, an urban area. Planning commissions and master plans for that area were deemed necessary (although contested) for their development. The County of Kauaʻi was attempting to establish that the Hui, whose Hāʻena lands were in a rural area, would have to submit to the process of subdivision in order to settle the suit.

In addition, in the arguments put forward in regards to this issue, the court recognized the *hui* to be a "peculiar or special Hawaiian institution." As long as there was a constitution or bylaws setting up governing procedures, a *hui* came into existence in the eyes of the law. This recognition is another example of how Hawaiian land laws are unique. The statues of Hawaiʻi on the subject of partition recognize *hui* and go to great lengths to preserve them and to facilitate the partitions of *hui* lands.

Another instance in which the courts recognized traditional customs and practices is found in the commissioners' report detailing the procedure of surveying the boundaries of land parcels bordering streams and storm drains. Boundaries of lands contiguous to waterways were run out to the middle of the drain or stream and conditions were set that all such lands be subject to the free flowage of water in all streams, drains, swales, and ancient ʻauwai (irrigation canals) and should enjoy water rights established by ancient usage. This understanding was coupled with an entitlement providing access for those people who used the water, enabling them to clean and maintain these ʻauwai, streams, and drains without liability on the owners of the land through which these waterways passed.

Further, the commissioners determined from all available data the areas of *kalo,* or "wet" lands. They recommended that these lands be declared to be entitled to water for *kalo* or similar culture. All surplus water not exhausted by reasonable seepage, evaporation, and the like was to be returned to the stream from which it was diverted at the rate of 15,000 gallons per day, per acre.

HOW THEY SLICED THE PIE

In determining how the division of the *hui* lands would be finalized, the great weight of Euro-American-inspired institutions of law and justice prevailed. Small skirmishes over ownership, land use, and access to resources erupted from time to time in the years following the partition. Yet the land as one sees it today is a result of the suit for partition completed more than forty years ago (see Hā'ena Ahupu'a Partition map on pages 116–117).

Because of the great variation in land found in Hā'ena *ahupua'a,* it was decided that the partition would be made on cash value rather than on the basis of area. The value of one whole share in the Hui Kū'ai 'Āina o Hā'ena was determined to be $11,612.77. Family members were allowed to combine their shares in order to preserve prior allotments or to obtain a more sizable parcel.

As mentioned earlier, the land was conveyed to the county for a well site and other necessities for providing water service to the community. Three other lots (131, 132, 133) were also awarded to the county based on the understanding that shareholders of the *hui* would be permitted to use rock and other material on those lots for fill purposes on their own lots within the Hā'ena Hui lands. However, these uses would be subject to reasonable rules of the county relating to manner, time, nature, and so on of such removal of such material. Deeds to other lots (44, 123, 128, 129, and the *heiau/hula* grounds in 121) awarded to the county contained a condition prohibiting concessions or commercial activities on any of the said lots.

The state reduced its concerns in regard to two particular issues: the location of School Grant 41 and the location of the common boundary of Hā'ena and the state-owned lands of Hanakapī'ai, the neighboring *ahupua'a* to the west.

Four lots (5, 6, 7, 42) remained unawarded to any person and were therefore offered at auction to shareholders at upset prices set forth by the commissioners in their reports. The upset prices were fairly low as evidenced by the actual prices paid by the successful bidders. Most opening bids were just above the upset prices. However, the court proceedings describe the bidding as being "spirited." Lot 42 was valued at $3,613.61 and the opening bid was for $3,614. The successful final bid made by Samson Mahuiki was for $15,501.00. Most lots were sold for three to five times their upset price. Fees raised by the sale of these lands were used to defray the costs of the court, commissioners, and guardians (attorneys) appointed by the court.

The commissioners were paid $17,000.00 in total. Norito Kawakami was paid $750.00 as guardian-ad-litem. Pratt, Moore, Bortz & Case were awarded $12,500.00, and $37,062.73 covered appraisers, surveyors, and miscellaneous charges properly incurred in connection with the proceedings. Expenses totaling $85,994.10 were incurred as the cost of the partition, excluding receipts from the four lots that were sold. Any other proper expenses thereafter incurred were taxed as costs against all of the parties listed as owning interests in the Hui pro-rated on a per share basis paid to the commissioners. John Gregg Allerton (who had had his name changed legally from John W. Gregg) and Paul G. Rice were credited with any money advanced by them to the commissioners from time to time in order to defray running expenses incurred by the commissioners as approved by the court.

All shareowners additionally owed adjusting payments. They had sixty days from the date of the final decree to pay the sum to the commissioners. The costs included the finalization of the surveys, the marking of the lands by survey pins, and the metes and bounds descriptions drawn up by the surveyors. In the event anyone failed to pay, they would be remanded to the court for appropriate order. Expenses of recording all deeds and any other incidental expenses had to be borne by the awardee or allottee in each case.

Table 4 lists the awardees in alphabetical order, along with the lot numbers and values attached to the lots at the time of the partition.

With the completion of the suit for partition, the lands of Hā'ena were finally entirely privatized. This *ahupua'a,* which for close to two thousand years had provided a wealth of resources extending from the mountains out into the sea, cultivated and shared by an entire community, was now fragmented and parceled out. In time, it would become, in a great number of cases, a site for vacation rentals, second homes for wealthy citizens from a far away continent, and residences for those with considerable access to monetary resources. Few aboriginal people have managed to hold on to their landholdings. These remnants of the original Native population persist in the face of ever climbing real property taxes fueled by speculative development and "flip that house" mentality. However, within surviving families, the skills of traditional fishermen and farmers, the stories passed down from many generations, and a unique sense of humor and identity rooted and nurtured in the special place that is Hā'ena continue to be manifested.

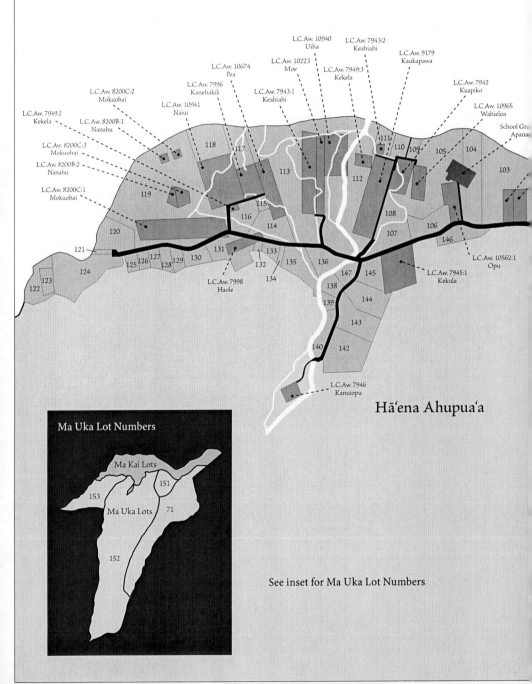

Hā'ena Ahupua'a Partition
ASSESSED IN 1965

L.C.Aw. 10940
Uiha

L.C.Aw. 7943:2
Keahiahi

L.C.Aw. 9179
Kaukapawa

L.C.Aw. 10674
Pea

L.C.Aw. 10223
Moe

L.C.Aw. 7949:3
Kekela

L.C.Aw. 7942
Kuapiko

L.C.Aw. 7996
Kanehakili

L.C.Aw. 7943:1
Keahiahi

L.C.Aw. 10965
Wahieloa

L.C.Aw. 8200C:2
Mokuohai

L.C.Aw. 10941
Naiui

School Gra
Apana

L.C.Aw. 7949:2
Kekela

L.C.Aw. 8200B:1
Nanahu

L.C.Aw. 8200C:3
Mokuohai

111

110   109   105   104

L.C.Aw. 8200B:2
Nanahu

118   117

113

112   103

L.C.Aw. 8200C:1
Mokuohai

115

119   108

116   114   107   106

120   146

121

125 126 127 128 129 130   131   133   135   136

L.C.Aw. 10562:1
Opu

124   132   134   147   145

L.C.Aw. 7998
Haole

138   144   L.C.Aw. 7945:1
Kekula

123
122   139

143

140   142

L.C.Aw. 7946
Kanuiopu

Hā'ena Ahupua'a

Ma Uka Lot Numbers

Ma Kai Lots

151

153   71

Ma Uka Lots

152

See inset for Ma Uka Lot Numbers

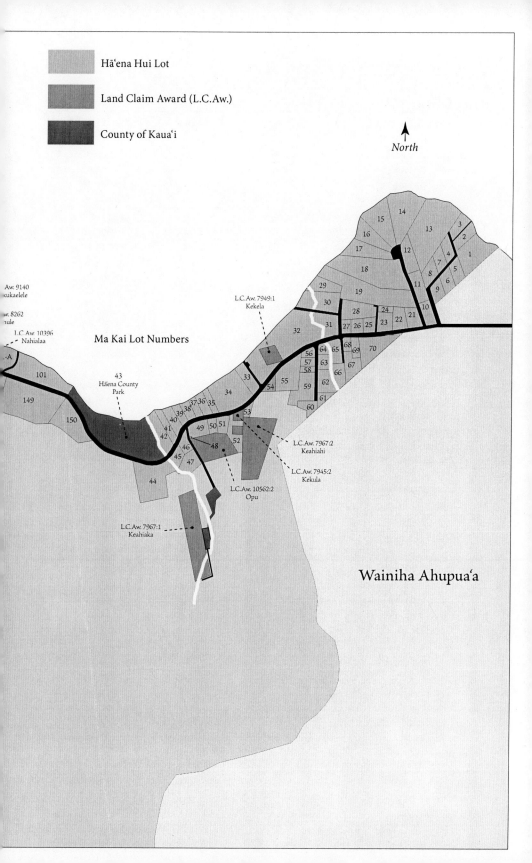

Hāʻena Hui Lot

Land Claim Award (L.C.Aw.)

County of Kauaʻi

North

Aw. 9140
kukaelele

w. 8262
nule

L.C.Aw. 10396
Nahialaa

-A

Ma Kai Lot Numbers

L.C.Aw. 7949:1
Kekela

L.C.Aw. 7967:2
Keahiahi

L.C.Aw. 7945:2
Kekula

L.C.Aw. 10562:2
Opu

L.C.Aw. 7967:1
Keahiaka

43
Hāʻena County
Park

Wainiha Ahupuaʻa

Table 4

Name	Lot #	Value of Lot
Aki Estate & Medeiros Estate	66	$2,539.61
John Allerton	32	$3,614.03
John Allerton	33	$23,269.88
John Allerton	53	$1,029.78
John Allerton	113	$15,980.69
John Allerton	121	$100.00
John Allerton	122	$12,263.23
John Allerton	153	$170.00
Sam Apo & Hazel Gross	65	$2,200.03
William & Patsy Asing	28	$1,105.38
Adolf Bartels, George Bartels, Alma B. Kealoha, Harriet B. Mariani, Helene B. Suganuma	67	$1,388.80
Rachel M. Bickel, Joseph Malia, William K. Malia, Caroline M. Nakamoto	61	$2,640.02
Beryl D. Bruhn, David Huddy, Dwight Huddy, James Huddy, Charla H. Lum, Harriet Yoshino	64	$2,202.02
William & Rosalina Chandler	29	$4,226.24
William & Rosalina Chandler	31	$6,033.13
William & Rosalina Chandler	126	$716.51
William & Rosalina Chandler	127	$420.00
Charles Chu	112	$3,630.87
William Chu & Chu Wai	2	$2,470.87
William Chu & Chu Wai	110	$1,784.81
William Chu & Chu Wai	111	$1,846.44
William Chu & Chu Wai	115	$1,507.00
Mildred Chung	50	$1,559.57
Dora Jane Cole	9	$1,697.60
Dora Jane Cole	26	$1,618.11
Dora Jane Cole	51	$3,112.10
Dora Jane Cole	46	$1,444.24
Dora Jane Cole	135	$2,140.69
Dora Jane Cole	136	$2,885.01
County of Kauaʻi	43	$20,098.51
County of Kauaʻi	44	$100.00
County of Kauaʻi	120	$273.76
County of Kauaʻi	123	$720.16
County of Kauaʻi	124	$792.00
County of Kauaʻi	125	$804.25
County of Kauaʻi	128	$100.00
County of Kauaʻi	129	exchange

Table 4 *(cont'd)*

Name	Lot #	Value of Lot
County of Kauaʻi	130	$100.00
Kamala De Fries, Ben Kanealiʻi, David Kanealiʻi,		
Joseph Kanealiʻi, Michael Kanealiʻi, Sam Kanealiʻi	62	$1,337.02
Helen R. Ellis & Wayne E. Ellis	10	$857.36
Helen R. Ellis & Wayne E. Ellis	16	$488,132.00
Helen R. Ellis & Wayne E. Ellis (one-fifth of)	20	$128.00
Helen K Ellis	30	$3,535.66
Michael L. Ellis	45	$1,585.89
Wayne R. Ellis	47	$2,320.81
Mary Ellis	3	$2,090.83
Mary Ellis	114	$2,900.50
Wayne E. Ellis	138	$1,443.57
Myra Gloss (Dower)	24	$784.98
A. Lindsay Faye, Jr.	60	$1,103.36
A. Lindsay Faye, Jr.	146	$448.57
Joe & Dora Hashimoto	69	$5,668.24
Elmer Keahi, Joseph Keahi, Norman Keahi,		
Raymond Keahi, Winona K. Rosehill	41	$2,561.63
Elmer Keahi, Joseph Keahi, Norman Keahi,		
Raymond Keahi, Winona K. Rosehill	137	$1,500.03
F. C. & Jenny Kling	104	$3,152.23
Maria Laʻamea, Victoria Lindsey, Claire Bukoski Follner	117	$4,346.64
John & Helen Lee	59	$1,437.84
Elizabeth Chandler, Marie Inouye, Bernard Mahuiki,		
Donald Mahuiki, Jeremiah Mahuiki, Lawrence Mahuiki,		
Ruth Mahuiki, Samson Mahuiki	58	$4,413.84
Murphy Maka, Helena Santos, Marjorie M. Yokotake,		
Hilda M. Zaima	54	$5,489.72
Chris Makaila	63	$936.20
Maile Montervon	57	$665.79
Howard H. Moore & Mary May Moore	105	$6,026.56
Howard H. Moore & Mary May Moore	106	$443.00
Howard H. Moore & Mary May Moore	108	$349.50
Polly Moore	107	$1,171.07
William & Jean Moragne	37	$2,228.17
William Moragne Jr.	39	$1,637.11
Jean Mary Cooke	40	$1,393.04
Sally Ann Moragne	38	$1,696.90
Catherine Moragne	36	$1,652.24
Robert Morton	139	$1,457.68

Table 4 *(cont'd)*

Name	Lot #	Value of Lot
Adeline Ogawa	56	$973.36
Emma Ouye	102	$4,178.67
Phyllis Ragsac	68	$1,357.92
Charles Rice Estate	134	$100.00
Edward & Martha Rice	18	$14,553.28
Edward & Martha Rice	(one-tenth of) 20	$64.00
Paul G. Rice	22	$2,365.86
Paul G. Rice	116	$1,057.85
Paul I. & Joyce Rice	19	$14,118.49
Paul I. & Joyce Rice	(one-tenth of) 20	$64.00
Richard K. Rice	8	$1,982.96
William Harrison Rice	12	$3,015.04
William Harrison Rice	14	$8,240.40
William Harrison Rice	(one-fifth of) 20	$128.00
William Harrison Rice	109	$1,120.33
A. Robinson Estate	34	$3,580.20
A. Robinson Estate	70	$25,060.79
A. Robinson Estate	118	$34,054.61
Eleanor Robinson	35	$11,837.32
Selwyn Robinson	119	$7,968.98
Agnes Thronas, Fred Thronas, Sam Thronas	49	$1,081.71
John Steelquist	11	$2,727.36
Bertha Tom	55	$963.27
Francelia K. Veech	15	$7,120.58
Francelia K. Veech	(one-fifth of) 20	$128.00
Wai'oli Hui'ia	23	$2,496.98
Dora Wallis	17	$6,081.51
Dora Wallis	(one-fifth of) 20	$128.00
Dora Wallis	21	$1,591.04
Dora Wallis	27	$1,522.35
Dora Wallis	48	$2,467.62
Charles Wichman	147	$624.03
Juliet Wichman	101	$5,123.39
Juliet Wichman	103	$7,593.08
Juliet Wichman	140	$2,054.40
Juliet Wichman	141	$2,375.76
Juliet Wichman	142	$2,891.02
Juliet Wichman	143	$2,408.68
Juliet Wichman	144	$2,288.80
Juliet Wichman	145	$2,424.92

Table 4 *(cont'd)*

Name	Lot #	Value of Lot
Juliet Wichman	148	$1,322.77
Juliet Wichman	149	$2,778.07
Juliet Wichman	150	$1,406.20
Juliet Wichman	151	$100.00
Juliet Wichman	152	$8,165.00
Gaylord Wilcox & Alice W. Sheehan	1	$7,880.21
Winifred Willis	4	$1,719.36
Winifred Willis	13	$16,845.21

Paʻitulu Kulupepee

Paʻitulu he made 'um (the canoe) himself, that old man. That old man never bother nobody, nobody. He make just one little paddle, only him. Only him was like that. Oh that old man and his home nothing when sleep, he sleep on the sand, he lay his mat, everything Hawaiian. Old style. And when he going catch fish, he not going tell you, he just go himself. With his canoe. Get on his canoe and go across Makua. He know the water, he know when to go, he don't tell nobody, 'cause he just go himself. Even in nighttime, he go with his fishing pole and go himself. Yeah, that old man. Ahhh, Paʻitulu! There's a picture of him at home and one by his canoe in the museum. NANCY MALIA PIʻILANI

Photograph by Helen H. Roberts, circa 1923, Bishop Museum.

CHAPTER SIX

KŪPUNA

 CHANGES OVER THE LAST two hundred years have been many and complex. Hāʻena, once a land supporting a robust population of agriculturalists, fisher folk, experts in chant and dance, and artisans producing from the abundance around them everything necessary for survival and prosperity, now is almost unrecognizable as such. First slowly, and then precipitously, Native ways of being in the world have been submerged by European, American, and Asian sensibilities, ethics, and aesthetics. After a catastrophic population collapse following first contact with Europeans, Americans, and those from other continents, the Native population slowly declined, becoming almost invisible. Although a great many are alienated from lands and continue to be challenged by an alien economic system, Native people survive. Throughout the time when independence as citizens of a sovereign nation was done away with and fisheries providing food and medicine were condemned by a government not of their choosing, Native people persist. Escalating real property taxes drove many from their lands, replacing them with people from other lands having more monetary wealth, yet some continued to hold fast to lives, lands, and identities.

A metaphor for the situation enjoyed by descendants of the Native people can be found in the *loʻi* lands, once full of water and nodding taro leaves, now standing idle, overgrown by invasive alien species overrunning and fracturing stone-faced terraces built by ancestors in millennia past. Still, these walls built and used by generations of ancestors remain a constant reminder to the aboriginal people of what existed in the time of the ancestors. Like the ancient stone walls still standing among the invading aliens, *kūpuna* and their families remain in Hāʻena, a living link to the world of the ancestors for present generations.

In its most common usage the word *kūpuna* refers to one's ancestors, grandparents, or relatives or close friends of the grandparents' generation. However, it can also mean starting point, source, or growing. *Kū* means to stand. One meaning for the word *puna* is spring (of water). Given these diverse levels of meaning, recognition of elders as wellsprings of knowledge and information standing among the people today provides an inspiration for younger generations. *Kūpuna* are living roots binding indigenous people firmly to island homelands and to more far-flung islands touched by distant ancestors over millennia. In Hāʻena, *kūpuna* of both the past and present continue to be an important source of growth, inspiration, guidance, and wisdom to present-day generations.

*Limahuli stream, now known as
the "cold pond" where the* keiki
*learned to swim. Photograph by
Piliāmoʻo © 2002.*

PERSONAL GLIMPSES

Although not born in Hā'ena, I spent many days and weeks there during my childhood, youth, and young adulthood. My father helped move a beachfront house back onto its foundations after the tidal wave of 1946. It had been picked up off the ground, turned around 180 degrees, and floated intact a hundred yards or so inland, where it was set down in a tangle of debris and *hau,* an indigenous variety of hibiscus. The owner, in reciprocation for my father's assistance, permitted our family to use the house for several weeks each year for many years.

Throughout the 1950s, going to Hā'ena seemed like an adventure into an exotic country. There, it seemed as if time had slowed itself down, at least up until the influx of greater and greater numbers of "flower children" searching for alternative lifestyles in the middle and late 1960s. In the early 1950s, the land was still held communally (pre-partition). Cows and horses roamed freely throughout the *ahupua'a.* People protected their home sites with fences to keep animals from damaging possessions, plants, and vegetable gardens. Automobile traffic, almost nonexistent by today's standards, often stopped as animals meandered onto roadways going about the daily round of grazing and seeking water. Often, they were heard at night, cropping *mānienie* and other grasses close under open windows of sleeping households who had forgotten to close the gates to the home compound. The only time these animals seemed to move with any spirit was when someone approached with rope in hand seeking to catch a horse for work or transportation. Or, as in the case of the cattle, whenever someone astride a horse approached, it usually signaled either a roundup or that someone needed some fresh meat. In this case, cattle would bolt for the nearby brush-covered ravines and hills.

On summer evenings after long days fishing, combing beaches, and rambling over animal trails, our father told stories about *mo'o* (lizard) and *manō* (shark), physical manifestations of ancestral guardians. He told of times gone by when his grandfather worked cattle on this, what seemed at the time, remote end of the island. He recounted stories, passed down in the family, of drives bringing wild cattle from remote valleys in the Nā Pali district into Hā'ena. His grandfather, Apelahama Hulilani Hobbs, was among the early cowboys herding these restless beasts over eleven miles of precipitous trails from Kalalau to the terminus of the government road at Kē'ē.

My father recalled being brought to Hā'ena as a child by his mother to visit relatives, and was familiar with the older Hawaiian families and other longtime residents of the area. He related stories of mountains, valleys, streams, and seas, cautioning that care be taken especially with the sea that during the winter season could change from what seemed a serene, glassy lake into a raging cauldron of twenty-foot-plus waves in a matter of a few hours. He described beings and persons who lived far in our ancestral past and whose places in Hā'ena we should respect and treat with care.

Later, during that period of life Tahitian relations call *tau re'are'a,* the time
of seeking youthful pleasure, I would come to know Hā'ena more intimately.
During those years, I lived in Hā'ena in different places and for varying periods
of times as surfing and other seasons designated. Friends from O'ahu allowed me
to stay in an old house when they were not there. They rented it from a Hā'ena
family as a vacation getaway. The old pine board and galvanized roofed house
huddled in a shadowy grove of immense Indian almond trees a short way down
an unpaved lane away from the paved main highway. I often stayed there alone.

Doors to the house would sometimes unexplainably open and close of their own
accord during the night. "It must be the wind or a faulty latch!" my more scientifi-
cally minded friends would counsel. Locals, however, related that it was just friendly
spirits walking through. Evidently, the house had been built on what used to be an
old path used by the people of olden times in their daily treks to the beach areas.

Walks at night led down the road winding through groves of trees, sometimes
emerging to pass closely along the sea and in turn burrow into the shadows of
nearby coastal cliffs. On these nights, currents of hot and cold air often material-
ized to whisper across skin. It was during these times the phrase "making your
hair stand on end" became a reality to me. These feelings were not manifestations of fear. Nonetheless, they were peculiar sensations, hair rising slowly on
the nape of the neck and continuing up the middle scalp until hair above the
forehead tingled with electricity.

Shortly after those years, Hā'ena went through readily discernable changes.
Cow and horse herds were put behind barbed wire in the mid-1960s. A large
land section, an area containing significant storied places, was condemned by
state government for use as a public park. Native families were evicted. Alien
trees, shrubbery, and other noxious vegetation soon covered lands after those
who had farmed the stone wall terraced fields were gone, compelled to vacate
land cultivated for centuries.

When I was thirty, it was in Hā'ena that I met the woman who would eventually become my wife. In Hā'ena our first child spent the initial year of his life in a
gardener's cottage next to Limahuli stream, learning to swim there almost before
he could walk. Although we left Hā'ena to take up residence on family land in the
Ko'olau district, continuing visits to Hā'ena in Halele'a, calling on friends, working with the people, and seeking the thrill of the challenging surf there increased,
strengthened, and nourished relationships with this special place. Two siblings
followed our firstborn, all of them learning to swim in the pond at Limahuli near
the cottage we had occupied formerly. Intervening years brought more contact
with *kūpuna* of Hā'ena working to restore abandoned *lo'i* to their former use.
It was during these times spent together that *kūpuna* shared memories of times
past. Some have passed away in the intervening years and some remain, but their
stories keep the memories of life in this special place alive.

George Kaʻeo on the rodeo circuit in his forties.
Dan Kaʻeo collection.

GEORGE KAʻEO

As mentioned earlier, in Hāʻena, cattle and horses were allowed to roam freely across the land. This was also true of other districts on Kauaʻi during the time when George Kaʻeo was a youth. Cattle and horses belonging to many owners roamed throughout the hinterlands of Hāʻena, sometimes straying into neighboring districts as well. In Hāʻena, particularly after it was acquired by the Hui Kūʻai ʻĀina o Hāʻena, all shareholders were allowed to graze a certain number of animals on the common lands, those not under cultivation or being used for house lots. Horses and cattle were used for transportation and meat and as beasts of burden, and had become essential to the life ways of the people since being introduced by early European explorers and entrepreneurs.

Kaʻeo, a Hawaiian cowboy, eighty some odd years old in the 1980s, was still an active horseman, training quarter horses and tutoring young *paniolo* (Hawaiian cowboys) in the arts of arena roping. He also worked as a wrangler for movie companies. Although he was well known in international polo circles, his roots were in Hāʻena. He told stories of riding cows into Nā Pali from Hāʻena during

*When Kaʻeo told me he had
ridden cows in Hāʻena and the
Nā Pali district, I thought he
was spinning a tall story. Later
my research uncovered these
photos of what was a common
place use for cattle in the early
historic period of Hāʻena.
Photograph by Alfred Mitchell,
1892, Bishop Museum.*

his youth, guiding them by tapping them on their horns with a stick. He claimed these mounts were better than horses at negotiating narrow cliff trails because of their placid dispositions. They were excellent at making their way through streams and swampy areas because their cloven hooves were less likely to get stuck in the mud. At the time he told me those stories, it seemed as if he was spinning yarns for my entertainment. Riding cows! Whoever heard of such a thing! Years later, while searching through collections of old photographs in the local museum, old black-and-white photos revealed images of men riding cattle in Hā'ena.

Ka'eo recounted activities that took place in seasonal roundups for branding cattle and horses of Hā'ena. Men folk, as well as relatives, friends, and interested parties from other districts, gathered there. The coastal plain was then open grassland. Only a few trees stood in sparse clumps scattered here and there. Hā'ena had not yet been invaded by the numerous, introduced, invasive species of trees and shrubs that transformed it into the forest standing there today. A few living *kūpuna* recall being able to see from near Maniniholo Cave all the way to Kepuhi point well beyond the eastern boundary of Hā'ena *ahupua'a*.

During these roundups, men, boys, and dogs scattered out into overgrown, brush-tangled nearby valleys and uplands searching out and driving cattle and

The coastal plain of Hā'ena where cattle were gathered and branded.
Photograph by Ray Jerome Baker, circa 1915, Bishop Museum.

horses onto the open coastal plain, where they were gathered into a big, milling herd. Branding fires were lit on the perimeter. Unbranded calves were roped by circling *paniolo* and dragged one by one to the fires, where brands of many different owners glowed bright red. When a bawling calf was dragged to the fire, the mother, reacting to the cry of her offspring, would run to its rescue. The men would then know the appropriate brand to apply.

When all unbranded animals in Hāʻena had been rounded up, branded, and released, younger men and others wanting to continue the adventure would ride to neighboring *ahupuaʻa,* gathering a herd there to begin the process over again. In district after district the traveling roundup made its way around the island until all the animals had been branded. According to Kaʻeo, many a romance

The caption emblazoned on George Kaʻeo's cap reads "Cowboys make better lovers." Dan Kaʻeo collection.

was instigated and new family connections begun during these times as young men made their way through communities far from their own, continuing a long tradition of widespread family bonds uniting families throughout the islands. Kaʻeo stayed active with horses and younger women well into his nineties. He is one who has gone to be with the ancestors.

SAMSON KAPAE MAHUIKI

Among Samson Kapae Mahuiki's earliest memories was the daily activity of working in the taro fields with his elders and being placed aboard the family horse along with the bags of taro to be taken from the fields to their home, close to a mile away. The large but gentle stallion used by the family was turned loose with Samson aboard to make his way home along the trails, lanes, and open areas separating fields from house lot. Unguided by the young boy, the wise old steed would make his way to the home compound, where women of the household would unload the taro and begin the task of preparing it for consumption by the extended family. Here, the taro was cleaned, cooked, and processed into *poi,* the daily "bread" of the community. A large container filled with taro and water would be set over a wood-burning fireplace, where it would boil and steam for many hours. The container was usually left to cool overnight so the cooked taro could be handled and the skins removed in preparation for pounding it into delicious and highly nutritious *poi*.

Samson made his living as a fireman at a time when there were no helicopters to perform rescues along the precipitous coastline beyond the end of the road. Nor were there any special rescue squads with extra training and special equipment. Samson, an avid hunter for most of his youth and well into his middle years, was very familiar with the mountainous areas of Hāʻena and the adjoining Nā Pali district. Astride his big, black stallion, enshrouded in rain gear, he would often answer the emergency call from the district headquarters, heading out into the dead of a stormy night to retrieve lost or overdue hikers. In most cases, these were strangers to the island who had bitten off more than they could chew in attempting to hike and camp in this district devoid of roads and other civilized amenities. When asked how he was able to negotiate the challenging and dangerous terrain in such demanding conditions, he confessed to often being unable to see the narrow trail during these rescues, trusting his horse to pick its way unguided by reins on these missions to find stranded hikers.

Samson, active in church, community, music and the land is a true patriarch. Although, often at repose or seeming to move at a leisurely pace, his mind is as agile as ever, as he reigns over his clan, constantly solving practical problems and finding easier ways to get difficult tasks done.

The ancient connection between the people of Hāʻena and Nā Pali district was one of longstanding duration. A unique, practical, reciprocal relationship evolving in historic times joined Hāʻena people and residents of the isolated valley of Kalalau, located at the end of the eleven-mile-long trail leading deep into Nā Pali. Kalalau valley, once home to a thriving population numbering well into the hundreds, continued to support a small community of permanent residents until the early 1900s. The fertile valleys of Nā Pali were somewhat more isolated from the rest of the island in post-contact times. They were only accessible by a narrow trail alternately winding itself in and out of the valleys, clinging to precipitous sea cliffs. During the relatively calm months of summer, a few select places could be accessed by sea. An incredible number of stone wall terraced fields are found in these valleys, now devoid of any permanent human residents. The extensive complexes of wall terraced fields and accompanying intricate system of ʻauwai (irrigation channels) are in some places reminiscent of the spectacular, highly terraced rice-growing complexes of pond fields found in China, the Philippines, and Indonesia still in use today. The ancient stone-faced terraces of Nā Pali stand in mute testimony to the industry of the people and the intense cultivation of those valleys in pre-Euro-American times.

Samson shared a little-known story illustrating how people of Kalalau and Hāʻena, in those early times, took advantage of the habits of their horses to facilitate the delivery of goods from one community to another. In those times, horses were an important means of everyday transportation. They were also all-important for working cattle and moving goods about. They were saddled and tied up next to the residents' homes every morning. If it was necessary for someone to go anywhere beyond reasonable walking distance, a horse would be available and ready to go. This meant that no time was ever wasted searching the neighborhood for an available mount. Sometimes the horses were released to graze with the rest of the herd roaming the *ahupuaʻa,* or they might be kept staked out nearby to graze but still available for use the next day. Because the horses were saddled and tied in the same place every day, they knew that they would be relieved of saddle and bridle when they entered the yard late in the day and stood at the spot where they were tied up daily. The animal-wise, practical, commonsense Hāʻena people took advantage of this habit when making their journeys to Kalalau in the neighboring Nā Pali district.

Hāʻena residents would, from time to time, go into the valleys of Nā Pali on excursions, hunting feral goats and fishing the less intensely used areas there. The people of Kalalau raised their own horses and kept them in their valley, utilizing them in much the same manner as the people in Hāʻena. Visitors from Hāʻena would often stay several days and sometimes a week or more on these jaunts. Often, quantities of fish or goat meat would be accumulated early on and would be ready to be sent home before the hunting party was ready to leave. There were no stores in Kalalau but in Wainiha, the neighboring *ahupuaʻa* east of Hāʻena, was a store stocked with kerosene, flour, and canned goods—items that had either become necessities or welcomed as luxuries, providing a change from the traditional diet of fish and *poi.*

Lists of goods to be purchased for the Kalalau residents were collected and included with bundles of salted meat and dried fish being sent back to Hāʻena.

These were fastened onto the backs of the horses from Hāʻena, which were loaded up and turned loose to wend their way home over the winding eleven-mile trail. Inevitably, they would make straight for their habitual tethering spot in the family compound, knowing it was only then they would be able to rid themselves of the burdens fastened to their backs. When the horses arrived, the women, young children, and elders left at home would unload them to begin the work of processing and storing the meat and fish. The horses were then turned loose to graze on their home range, the common lands in Hāʻena. Lists from the Kalalau people fastened to the loads were taken to the store, where goods were purchased or gathered and made ready to be sent back to Kalalau.

Meanwhile, the men in Kalalau continued hunting and fishing. When they were finally ready to depart, they would borrow Kalalau horses, often those belonging to relatives who lived there, to ride home to Hāʻena. Upon arriving home, their new cargo would be unloaded and the Kalalau horses loaded with merchandise from the store as well as other gifts and supplies from the Hāʻena families. Kalalau horses, used to being unsaddled in front of their owners' homes in the valley, would return there, delivering the loads to that distant destination.

KAIPO CHANDLER

Kaipo Chandler worked as a cowboy for the Robinsons, a family originally from Scotland having large landholdings in Hāʻena and considerable acreage on the west side of Kauaʻi. The family purchased the entire island of Niʻihau in the mid-1800s. In Haleleʻa, they ran cattle in Hāʻena, Wainiha, Lumahaʻi, and Waipa, as well as in several valleys in the Nā Pali district. A compactly built, muscular, active, energetic man, Kaipo, now well into his eighties, told fascinating stories about his experiences working cattle there.

The once open grassy valleys of Nā Pali are now overgrown with alien species of plants run amok as in most of the lands in Hawaiʻi. Java plum trees, thorny lantana shrubs, and thickets of guava are just a few of the many non-native species introduced from foreign lands. As there were no corrals and very little flat, open ground available to gather a herd of the cattle in the valleys, cowboys caught them individually, beating the bushes and chasing them into the boulder-studded riverbeds, often the only places open enough to wield a rope. After being chased and roped, cattle were maneuvered in such a way as they could to be pinned to a tree. In order to accomplish this, the cowboy had to wrap the lariat around a tree and pull the beast up tight. He then had to dismount, get in close enough to tie the raging animal there with a shorter piece of rope kept for just that purpose, and disengage his lariat to repeat the process again with another animal. The riderless horse (or mule) had to be trusted to keep the tension on the lariat until the task was done. Mounts had to be well trained because loosening the tension would place the rider, now afoot, in danger of being seriously injured if the rope parted

Kaipo Chandler.
Photographs from the
Kaipo Chandler collection.

or the horse neglected its job. The caught animal would remain tied tightly to the tree fighting the rope, often for many hours. In the earliest years, captured bovines would then be tethered to tame bullocks, which would lead them out along the treacherous trail. In later years, the Robinsons acquired a surplus World War II landing craft. The cowboys would lead the cattle down to the beach, where they would be loaded aboard and carried by sea to market.

Mounts had to be nimble and quick witted enough to dodge charges, which happened more often than not with these wily and quick-tempered beasts. Kaipo recalled cattle in those days being much more aggressive than those of the present time. Most had long, sharp horns. Many were descended from Longhorns introduced from California and Mexico by early explorers eager to implant a source of meat for future voyages to these islands. He related that if they saw a

man on foot, these cattle would most certainly pursue him. This was especially true of cattle whose "blood was up" as a result of being harassed by men and dogs for sustained periods of time. Once, when caught afoot, Kaipo remembered scrambling up a relatively small guava tree to escape an irate cow that repeatedly battered the trunk, trying to dislodge and knock him the ground.

Another hair-raising moment happened when he was aboard his mule. Often cattle were caught in valleys and gulches far from the holding grounds located near the beach. When caught, they then needed to be led down narrow trails to join the herd being gathered for transport out of the valley. In most cases, in order to safely bring the cattle along the narrow, steep trails, one cowboy would lead the animal, another followed. Both had ropes attached to the horns. The one in front led the way, the one in the back acted as the brake, especially important on downhill sections of the trail.

On this particular occasion, the rear cowboy either lost or let go of his end of the rope. The freed animal charged and butted Kaipo's mount, lifting its hind legs completely off the ground. Kaipo, sitting precariously in the saddle, got the ride of his life on the mule, which managed to keep its footing but was propelled down the trail for several hundred yards with two forelegs pumping rapidly to keep from being run over by the angry animal behind. Kaipo and his mule miraculously escaped physically unscathed. But, as Kaipo chuckled in remembrance, forever after the incident, that particular mule would leap out of its skin if any cow made a sudden move toward it or even sneezed in its direction. If the rider were not alert, he would quickly be unseated.

Though he made his living as a ranch hand, Kaipo was also a fisherman, who on his boat would venture into the deep ocean for pelagic fish. He was a hunter, respected for his knowledge of mountain areas. In his youth, he once followed a man reputed to be a *kahuna* into the depths of Lumaha'i valley, where the storied Menehune lived in times gone by. The man's looks and reputation so intimidated Kaipo that he stayed well to the rear as the trek went deeper and deeper inland, beyond any place that Kaipo had explored on previous hunting forays. Eventually, Kaipo felt so uncomfortable, he turned around. He never went that deep into Lumaha'i again.

Kaipo enjoyed a having a good time with friends, and was one of few men who would launch into extemporaneous hula during parties and jam sessions. There was nothing effeminate about his interpretations of the traditional Hawaiian dance. He was cowboy, hunter, and fisherman, all rough and ready vocations, and yet he dared to hula, considered by some in those times a most unmasculine activity.

JOHN HANOHANO PĀ

In his younger years, Hanohano Pā saved the life of one member of a wealthy, local missionary family when he was swept out to sea in rising winter surf. The young man's father, a large landowner and important political leader on Kaua'i at the time, rewarded Hanohano Pā by appointing him community sheriff. John told this story himself, and other people tell it as well.

Nancy: My papa saved Philip Rice. Remember? I have the newspaper article. He got a gold watch for that. Oh that was 1920 something, you should see the sea was rough, rough, rough. I mean waves in Hā'ena by the Rice's place. Makua. The people didn't want my papa to go. They tell, "No go!" My tūtū lady said no go because the sea is too rough. My papa saved two of them. And who was the other one he had save beside Philip? A doctor. I have the story of my papa. My father's picture with Philip Rice, he is giving the gold watch and on top of that Papa got the boat.

Nancy Malia Pi'ilani.
Photograph by Hau'oli
Wichman, 2002.

All *kūpuna* attest that fishing was of primary importance to life in Hā'ena. Reefs there have always been "ice box," bank account, medicine chest, and retirement plan for the community. The reefs provide access to seafood even during the tumultuous winter season of giant waves. Additionally, the sheltering reef at Makua is a place for spawning aggregations of several types of fish during the calmer summer months, providing fish for immediate consumption and for drying for use in the winter months. In the years following the introduction of the market economy, the surplus of community nettings was often sold to fish peddlers and brokers for markets on the other side of the island.

Both men and women were skilled at different types of fishing. Men often were spear fishers as well as the primary handlers of the large nets. After the introduction of the throw nets, single fishermen or family groups would stalk feeding schools of fish on top of the fringing reefs during the ebb and flow of the tides. This diurnal rhythm dictated the movement of reef fish up onto shallow reef flats to feed on seaweed growing there and then retreating into deeper waters when the flats dried up.

As mentioned in earlier chapters, John Hanohano Pā was a prominent fisher-man during his lifetime. John's family was one of the last families to leave their initial home in Kalalau and move to the relatively less isolated community of Hāʻena. Here, he went to school and eventually earned a reputation for his prowess in the ocean. An important event elevating his status in the community was a heroic rescue he performed, saving a scion of a well-to-do missionary family from being lost at sea in rapidly rising waves generated by a distant winter storm. John, a tall, powerfully built man able to swim strongly well into his sixties, on that day swam out through and beyond the rising surf towing a rescue rope to the stranded man. For saving Philip Rice, John was appointed sheriff of the Hāʻena district. However, it was his character and excellence as a fisherman that most people remember about him.

It was said by the people of Hāʻena who remember him that fish would practically come up and present themselves to John at Makua in the lee of Hāʻena point, in front of the gardener's cottage where he was the caretaker and stored his nets and other fishing equipment. The reason he was such a successful fisherman, according to *kūpuna* living today, was that John always gave away his catch to the community until everyone had more than enough to eat and to dry. Only then, when no one needed any more fish for home consumption, would he notify the peddlers and fish brokers there was fish for sale. They say that the more he gave away, the more fish would come into the bay for him to catch. Although John owned the nets and boat used for setting the nets, it was the community that made it possible for the large nets to be deployed and maintained.

Keeping and maintaining nets required a lot more work than those made today of synthetic materials. The relatively fragile nets had to be spread out and dried thoroughly before being put away in the net shed so they would not rot or mildew. Community members helped spread the nets on the grassy lawns on sunny days after the fishing took place. Many elders and others who had the skill would spend time patching the inevitable holes appearing after each use of the nets.

As an owner of nets and several boats, Hanohano Pā also led many fishing expeditions to other places along the coast. He was especially famous for his familiarity with the Nā Pali district and for fishing in its many sea caves. He had lived there for a time in his youth as a member of one of the last Hawaiian families whose home was the Nā Pali district. Nancy Piʻilani, John's daughter, vividly remembered accompanying her father on these fishing trips. She shared her fear about having to swim into dark sea caves assisting with setting and retrieving the nets. He directed setting nets inside several sea caves spaced along the coast between Hāʻena and Kalalau in search of the elusive *moi* (threadfin), a highly prized and sought after delicacy. In time, he acquired a diesel-powered sampan and would often fish with younger men of the community or his children. He even took along his daughters, who had to pull their weight on these expeditions.

Nancy: He'd go swim all in those caves. Go set the net. To go set the net, they go swimming inside. They go inside and chase the moi *(threadfish—Polydactylus sexfilis) out in the bag. That time they used to use a bag (built especially for the net). It was the kind they go drag net. That's the kind. Drive, drive, drive (the fish) go, in the bag. They lift 'um up. He was a fisherman.*

One story about his ability as a waterman involved a famous yacht woman who had sailed from the continent. She had fouled her anchor in deep water off the beach at Kalalau. John, well into his sixties at the time, passing by on his boat stopped and dove down into water over sixty feet deep, without the aid of any artificial diving aids like fins or aqualung, freeing the anchor.

BARLOW CHU AND FAMILY

Other families in Hā'ena also trace their roots to the Nā Pali district. According to family documents, the Kinney family came to Hā'ena from Ireland by way of Connecticut. Early Kinneys were entrepreneurs, growing coffee in the Nā Pali district and sugar on Maui and Hawai'i. The Kinneys became Hawaiian by marrying Hawaiian women. William Kihapi'ilani Kinney lived in what was an unusual arrangement by today's standards, with Puaokina, a woman from Kalalau, Alika Hailama, another man, and Alapa'i, Kiha's first wife. Apparently, all got along well in this arrangement. Family members are not clear as to why Sarah, a daughter of Puaokina, was named Hailama, not Kinney.

> *Kū mai Hailama, pa'a i ka hoe*
> *i mua a i hope, ke kulana nei.*
>
> *(Hailama stands forth, firmly grasping the steering oar*
> *forward and backward [the rowing], in position.)*

The preceding lines are from an old song entitled "Hula o Makee" telling the story of the ship *Malulani,* wrecked on the reef at Kapa'a, on the eastern coast of Kaua'i in the 1800s. Hailama, a commanding figure whose bearing suggested someone of authority, well known as a boat steersman, was summoned from Hā'ena to assist in the rescue and salvage effort. Known in Hā'ena as a provider, he and Puaokina raised Sarah, feeding and mentoring children from other families as well. He was also one of the last people familiar with the very difficult trail leading to the top of Makana, the peak dominating the skyline of Hā'ena and from which the 'ōahi ceremony was conducted.

Sarah Hailama married a Chinese tailor, Chu Wai. Barlow Chu, a middle child, of these two very different individuals was a mentor of mine in the ways of Hā'ena. My earliest encounter with Barlow Chu was on an inky, dark night on the unlighted road leading from the trailhead at Ke'ē back toward civilization. Two friends and I had just stumbled out through the last two miles of the coastal trail barefoot and fatigued in darkness so intense you literally could not see the white T-shirt of the companion in front of you. Dragging down the pot-holed ridden road, we saw a car approach. It was surprising to see a car there because the old wooden Lumaha'i bridge, four or five miles away, had collapsed, leaving this end of the island unreachable by vehicles.

Apparently, this particular car was stranded on the Hā'ena side of the bridge when it collapsed and Barlow, a policeman, was assigned to keep the peace on the far side of the bridge in the land where he had spent his youth. Barlow, as was his way, stopped and offered us a ride. Once in the car, he took us to a house, fed us, and then delivered us to men operating rowboats transporting people across the river at the incapacitated bridge.

Charlie Chu entering his ninth decade. Photograph by Hau'oli Wichman, 2003.

Barlow was one of those talented, intelligent, generous people who embody the characteristics of true *kūpuna*. He was a teacher, a man skilled in the ways of the sea and the land, as well as a gifted musician who emulated the style and perpetuated the songs of the early composers and musicians of Halele'a. He was a living spring of knowledge about fishing, farming, traveling on the sea, and the idiosyncrasies of people and life. He shared his knowledge with *malihini* (strangers) and *kama'āina* (longtime residents) alike. Luckily, some of his music and impressions are preserved on audio- and videotapes recorded in his later years, after his retirement from the police force. He shared one facet of life in those years that was probably common to many families of marriages made between Native Hawaiians and those that came later. Barlow recalled his confusion and difficulty growing up in a time when the school systems suppressed the Hawaiian language and English was promoted as the only viable alternative for an education. In a family whose mother's first language was Hawaiian and whose father's was Chinese, the language of the school system and the law, English, put him and his siblings at a disadvantage in the area of communication. Both mother and father wanted to support their children's education, so they communicated in the home in English, a language in which neither was fluent nor comfortable. According to Barlow, it made for interesting family discussions. Among many of Barlow's memories was seeing the last traditional canoe used for fishing in Hā'ena.

Charlie and Barlow Chu playing the music of Halele'a. Presley Wann family collection.

Pa'itulu, a chanter of note whose voice is recorded on audiotapes collected by Bishop Museum anthropologists, was a relative of Barlow's family and owner of the canoe. Apparently, Pa'itulu was the last person practicing the art of subsistence fishing using traditional watercraft. The canoe disappeared one night. Barlow felt it might have been a tsunami big enough to take the canoe but not of the magnitude to come up onto the higher lands threatening and devastating the people as it did in later years. When asked what happened, Pa'itulu simply responded, "Nalu, nalu" (Wave, wave).

Barlow's grandparents raised his eldest brother Charles, who spent his entire youth in Hā'ena. At the time I was writing this book, he was in his nineties, living in Honolulu and still an active musician. A self-taught painter, he painted from memory, capturing the image of his boyhood home, remembering the time he spent with Hailama and Puaokina at the family homestead at Kamealoha (the beloved). He pointed out in his painting the wooden plank house surrounded by *lo'i* planted in *kalo* where Hailama raised him as well as other young people from the community. He also pointed out the little grass *hale,* one of the last of its kind in Hā'ena, which housed an elderly Hawaiian man, also cared for by Hailama and his family. Barlow has been gone for many years, after first having to sell his portion of the family land due to rising real property taxes. The remainder of the lands of Kamealoha are at risk today, brought about in large part by extremely high real property assessments the family can ill afford to pay.

THOMAS HASHIMOTO
From the time of his birth on July 13, 1934, in a small, wooden house in Hā'ena, Thomas Hashimoto was destined to be a fisherman. He was the fourth child of five born to Joe and Dora Hashimoto in what was then an isolated rural community near the end of the government road on the northwest shore of Kaua'i. His father had not lived in Hā'ena all his life. In fact, he was born in South Kona on the Big Island in a small village, Nāpō'opo'o. Joe's father, a Japanese immigrant,

after arriving on the Big Island had married a pure Hawaiian woman and raised his children speaking fluent Hawaiian. Many early immigrants did, as Hawaiian had not been outlawed and was still the first language of most of the population in Hawai'i at the time.

Like many young people, Joe decided to leave the place of his birth and seek opportunity elsewhere. His travels took him to several islands. Eventually, he sought out his uncle, Mahiula Keone, living in Hā'ena. Mahiula had also left Nāpō'opo'o years before and word had reached Joe that he was living in Hā'ena.

Joe soon found Hā'ena was to his liking and settled down to raise his family. In those days, tourists had not yet discovered Hawai'i, and Hā'ena was a small but healthy community of mostly Hawaiians with a few Japanese and Chinese mixed in, all of whom supplemented their very modest incomes with subsistence skills, growing taro and vegetables and catching fresh fish from the sea. It was in this isolated setting that Thomas grew up learning to fish and farm as soon as he could walk. In those days, walking was the primary mode of transportation and the walks to and from the family's *hale* (house) to their *lo'i kalo* (taro patches) and back were always filled with opportunities to pick fruit or catch fish.

Tom Hashimoto, farming and fishing actively well into his seventies. Photographs by Hau'oli Wichman, 2002.

Attending Hāʻena School, located about a mile-and-a-half from the Hashim-oto home near Makua beach, Thomas learned to read and write in English. At home his parents spoke Hawaiian only in private and with others of their generation. They discouraged their five children from speaking the Native language. Many of the parents of that time did so, in part because of legislation against the use of Hawaiian language and in part because they wanted their children to succeed in a world in which Euro-American language, values, and customs played a large role in providing access to better economic opportunities. In spite of this, Thomas listened and observed as his father spoke about and demonstrated the skills and knowledge accumulated through his own life experience and his relationship with the ocean areas of Hāʻena. An avid fisherman, Thomas absorbed as much as he could about the places where fish lived and the proper time to catch them.

Year after year he accompanied his father, who always referred by traditional Hawaiian names of the locations where the fish were caught. As Thomas got older, his father, having grown too old to endure the rigors of hunting fish on the reefs, would often ask him to go and look for particular kinds of fish at certain locations. Thomas, who had learned well the names of the ʻāpapa (reefs) of Hāʻena and other nearby districts, knew right where to go whenever fish were needed to feed his family or to contribute to family celebrations of birth, graduation, marriage, or the passing of a loved one. Thomas, masterful in knowing the ways of fish and their habits, also knew where the limu (seaweed) that was their food grew and what seasonal, tidal, and sea conditions were just right to capture them. As countless generations had before him, he had become intimate with the land and sea, using this knowledge to feed his family and share with others in the community.

In recent years Thomas was instrumental in providing many Hawaiian names along the reefs and seashore for a map compiled and constructed to preserve this legacy for generations to come. He continues to provide fish for his family, and he has mentored several younger men in the ancestral art of seeking out fish in and on the reefs that have provided sustenance to the people of Hāʻena for almost two thousand years.

Epilogue

Ha'ina 'ia mai ana ka puana,
aloha 'ia nō o Hā'ena e ka Hui Maka'āinana.

◊◊◊◊

Let the story be told.
Hā'ena is beloved by the people of the land.

In the singing of *mele* (the songs of these islands), the last verse often exhorts
those listening to join in and sing the refrain again along with the singers. As
mentioned earlier, Hā'ena is only one of many lands in Nā Kai 'Ewalu (the realm
of the eight seas), as Hawai'i was known to the people of old. Each has stories
embedded in land, sea, sky, and the lives of the people. Songs of these places are
chanted in winds, murmur in water, and resonate out of earth and stone. The
character of people is nourished by *'āina* and celebrated when conveyed from
generation to generation.

This story of Hā'ena grew out of affection *hoa'āina* have for places they
inhabit, bearing tribute to that which nourishes mind, body, and spirit and
continues to be the *kahua* (foundation) for identity. This story is by no means a
definitive portrayal of every aspect of life and spirit of Hā'ena. It is only a beginning, springing from a desire that younger generations will continue to seek out,
learn, restore, and perpetuate the legacy of ancestors whose bones lie beneath
sand and earth and rest in caves sprinkled throughout cliffs and mountains.

It is my desire that this story will serve to inform any who seek to know the
land more intimately. I also hope that *'ōiwi* (Native people) of other places in
Hawai'i will seek out their own storied places on the islands of their birth,
thereby strengthening their own connections to Papahānaumoku (Papa who
gives birth to islands), the earth mother, and to the sky father, Wakea (the broad
expanse of the heavens), and to our elder siblings, the islands themselves. As
ancestors recognized the power of *palapala* (the written word), it is hoped that
more Native people will celebrate their own *'āina* in print, seeking out and cher-
ishing the wisdom of *kūpuna,* those who have passed and those still standing
among us. We trust that these *keiki o ka 'āina* (children of the land) will retrace
their genealogical roots, rediscovering the *mana* it imbues to their own lives.
The anticipation is that these endeavors will provide a deeper conviction to *kia'i*
(stand guard over), that it will engender an enduring commitment to *mālama*

(care for) the *waiwai* (resources) of the *'āina*. And I hope that this story will foster an assurance to *onipa'a* (stand fast) for the *'āina* as those who came before us have done.

Pua Kanahele, *kumu hula* (teacher of traditional dance), *haku mele* (composer of songs and chants), and *alaka'i* (leader) of *kanaka maoli* who have accepted the *kuleana* (responsibility) to stand against the tide seeking to envelop, obscure, and eventually dispossess the Native people, has declared, that all of us are the manifestation of the places in which we live. When we learn and retell a story of the ancestors, sing a song about our places, and practice the skills and values passed on to us by our elders, we extend the life ways of our ancestors, prolonging the life and identity of our people into the time in which we live.

As our ancestors encountered many challenges discovering, settling upon, and passing through archipelagos to the south to arrive and flourish here in these northern seas, adapting to and overcoming each new test, so too can we adapt to and thrive in the places we inhabit today without giving up our unique identity as a people, despite being confronted by newer issues and challenges.

Regaining proficiency in our mother tongue despite the historical legacy of suppression and extending this rich inheritance of our ancestors through the vehicle of the written word is only one of many avenues of prolonging our birthright. One objective of this book is to encourage other *'ōiwi* to collect the wisdom, humor, adventure, and aspirations of their places, bringing them into the realm of *palapala* (books and documents), providing long living sources to satisfy the inquiries of their own descendants as well as to inform the curiosity of visitor and newcomer commemorating the wealth of *'āina*.

As for Hā'ena, the story continues. The *'āina* persists in revealing new aspects of its character as the searching continues and time is invested restoring the land. Uncovering historical maps brings names, long forgotten, back to light, giving them new life. Recurrent scanning of recovered Hawaiian-language newspaper collections reveals older times seen through Hawaiian eyes. Most important, frequent conversations and activities with *kūpuna* warm affections, strengthening links to *mo'o kū'auhau* (genealogy) stretching back more than two thousand years.

References

Akina, J. A. 1904. "He Moolelo No Ka Poe Menehune, i wae a hoonohonoho pono ia e like me ia i hai ia mai ka paa naau e na Elemakule o Waimea a hoea loa aku i Mana." Kauaʻi, Hawaiʻi. Unpublished manuscript.

Alexander, William De Witt. 1889. *A Brief Account of the Hawaiian Government Survey, its Objects, Methods and Results.* Honolulu: Honolulu Bulletin Steam Print.

Barrère, Dorothy B., Mary Kawena Pukui, and Marion Kelly. 1980. *Hula: Historical Perspectives.* Honolulu: Department of Anthropology, Bernice P. Bishop Museum.

Basso, Keith H. 1996. *Wisdom Sits in Places: Landscape and Language Among Western Apache.* Albuquerque: University of New Mexico Press.

Beckwith, Martha Warren. 1970. *Hawaiian Mythology.* Honolulu: University of Hawaiʻi Press.

———. 1972. *The Kumulipo, A Hawaiian Creation Chant.* Honolulu: University of Hawaiʻi Press.

Bennett, Wendall Clark. 1931. *Archaeology of Kauaʻi.* Millwood, N.Y.: Bernice P. Bishop Museum bulletin 80. Kraus Reprint Co.

Cannerola, L. 1974. *The Origins of Hawaii Land Titles and of the Rights of Native Tenants.* Honolulu: Security Title Corporation.

Chinen, Jon Jitsuzo. 1958. *The Great Mahele: Hawaii's Land Division of 1848.* Honolulu: University of Hawaiʻi Press.

———. 1971. *Original Land Titles in Hawaiʻi.* Honolulu: University of Hawaiʻi Press.

———. 2006. "The Hawaiian Land Revolution of the 1840s and 1850s." *Hawaiʻi Bar Journal* (July).

Daws, Gavan. 1968. *Shoal of Time: A History of the Hawaiian Islands.* Honolulu: University of Hawaiʻi Press.

Dole, Sanford B. 1892. "Evolution of Hawaiian Land Tenures." Paper presented to the Hawaiian Historical Society, December 5.

Dougherty, Michael. 1992. *To Steal a Kingdom: Probing Hawaiian History.* Waimanalo, Hawaiʻi: Island Style Press.

Earle, Timothy Keese. 1973. "Control Hierarchies in the Traditional Economy of Haleleʻa District, Kauaʻi." Ph.D. diss., University of Michigan.

Emerson, Nathaniel Bright. 1964. *Unwritten Literature of Hawaii: The Sacred Songs of the Hula.* Rutland, Vt., and Tokyo: Charles E. Tuttle Company.

———. 1978. *Pele and Hiʻiaka, A Myth from Hawaiʻi.* Rutland, Vt., and Tokyo: Charles E. Tuttle Company.

Emory, Kenneth Pike. 1929. "Ruins at Kē'ē, Hā'ena, Kaua'i." In *The Hawaiian Annual,* edited by Thos. G. Thrum, 88–94. Honolulu: Thos. G. Thrum.

Feher, Joseph. 1969. *Hawaii: A Pictorial History.* Honolulu: Bernice P. Bishop Museum Press.

Fitzpatrick, Gary L., and Riley M. Moffat. 1986. *Early Mapping in Hawai'i,* vol. I: *Palapala'āina.* Honolulu: Editions Limited.

———. 1995. *Surveying the Mahele,* vol. II: *Palapala'āina.* Honolulu: Editions Limited.

Fornander, Abraham. [1878–1885] 1969. *An Account of the Hawaiian Race.* Rutland, Vt., and Tokyo: Charles E. Tuttle Company.

———. [1919] 1999. *Fornander Collection of Hawaiian Antiquities and Folk-lore.* Honolulu: 'Ai Pōhaku Press.

Handy, Edward Smith Craighill, Elizabeth Green Handy, and Mary Kawena Pukui. 1972. *Native Planters in Old Hawai'i, Their Life, Lore, and Environment.* Honolulu: Bernice P. Bishop Museum Press.

Handy, Edward Smith Craighill, and Mary Kawena Pukui. 1977. *The Polynesian Family System in Ka'ū, Hawai'i.* Rutland, Vt., and Tokyo: Charles E. Tuttle Company.

Hau'ofa, Epeli. 2001. "Epilogue: Pasts to Remember." In *Remembrance of Pacific Pasts: An Invitation to Remake History,* edited by R. Borofsky. Honolulu: University of Hawai'i Press.

———. 1994 "Our Sea of Islands." *The Contemporary Pacific: A Journal of Island Affairs* 6, no. 1 (Spring).

Hawaii Department of Foreign Affairs. 1848. *Answers to questions proposed by His Excellency, R. C. Wyllie, His Hawaiian Majesty's Minister of Foreign Relations, and addressed to all the missionaries in the Hawaiian Islands, May 1846.* Honolulu.

Hawaii Land Commission. 1846. *Native Register, Native Testimony and Foreign Testimony,* Hawai'i State Archives.

———. Land Matters File. Documents n.d.–400. Hawai'i State Archives.

Hawaiian Studies Institute, Kamehameha Schools/Bishop Estate (KSBE). 1982. *The Ahupua'a.* Honolulu: Kamehameha Schools Press.

Henry, Teuira. [1847–1915] 1985. *Ancient Tahiti.* New York: Bernice P. Bishop Museum bulletin 48. Kraus Reprint Co.

Hooulumahiehie. 1906. "Ka Moolelo o Hiiaka-i-ka-poli-o-pele." *Ka Na'i Aupuni,* Buke II, Helu 1, Pō'alima, June 1, 1906–Buke II, Helu 155, Pō'alima, November 30, 1906.

Indices of Awards Made by the Board of Commissioners to Quiet Land Titles in the Hawaiian Islands. 1929. Honolulu: Office of the Commissioner of Public Lands, Territory of Hawai'i.

Kamakau, Samuel Manaiakalani. 1961. *Ruling Chiefs of Hawai'i.* Rev. ed. Honolulu: Kamehameha Schools Press.

———. 1964. *Ka Po'e Kahiko: The People of Old.* Honolulu: Bernice P. Bishop Museum Press.

———. 1976. *The Works of the People of Old, Na Hana a ka Poʻe Kahiko.* Honolulu: Bernice P. Bishop Museum Press.

———. 1992. *Ruling Chiefs of Hawaii.* Honolulu: Kamehameha Schools Press.

Kameʻeleihiwa, Lilikala. 1992. *Native Land and Foreign Desires/Pehea Lā E Pono Ai?* Honolulu: Bernice P. Bishop Museum Press.

Kanahele, George S. 1986a. *Kū Kanaka, Stand Tall: A Search for Hawaiian Values.* Honolulu: University of Hawaiʻi Press and Waiaha Foundation.

———. 1986b. *Waikīkī, 100 B.C. to 1900 A.D., An Untold Story.* Honolulu: The Queen Emma Foundation.

Kekahuna, H.E.P. 1959. Ka-ulu-a-Paoa Heiau, Kēʻē, Hāʻena, Kauaʻi. Brief Descriptive Notes, Ground Plan, and Elevation.

Kelly, Marion. 1956. "Changes in Land Tenure in Hawaiʻi, 1778–1850." Master's thesis, University of Hawaiʻi.

———. Results of the Great Mahele of 1848 and the Kuleana Act of 1850. Unpublished manuscript.

———. 1989. "Dynamics of Production Intensification in Precontact Hawaiʻi." In *What's New? A Closer Look at the Process of Innovation,* edited by Sander van der Leeuw and Robin Torrence, 82–106. London: Unwin Hyman.

Kepelino, Z. 1932. *Kepelino's Traditions of Hawaiʻi.* Ed. Martha Beckwith. Millwood, N.Y.: Bernice P. Bishop Museum bulletin 95. Kraus Reprint Co.

Kimura, Larry. 1983. *Native Hawaiian Culture.* Native Hawaiian Study Commission Report. Vol. I. Washington, D.C.: U.S. Department of the Interior.

King, Robert Davis. 1942. *Hawaiian Land Titles.* Reproduced through the courtesy of the Honolulu Board of Realtors. Source of materials: [Hawaii (Ter.) Bureau of Real Property] appraisal manual for assessors and appraisers of real property [1942].

Kosaki, Richard H. 1954. *Konohiki Fishing Rights.* Honolulu. Report No. 1 (request No. 3642). Legislative Reference Bureau, University of Hawaiʻi.

Kuykendall, Ralph S. 1938. *The Hawaiian Kingdom, 1778–1854.* Vol. I. Honolulu: University of Hawaiʻi Press.

Lam, M. 1985. "The Imposition of Anglo-American Land Tenure Law on Hawaiians." *Journal of Legal Pluralism and Unofficial Law* no. 23.

———. 1989. "The Kuleana Act Revisited: The Survival of Traditional Hawaiian Commoner Rights in Land." *Washington Law Review* 64, no. 2.

Levy, Neil M. 1975. "Native Hawaiian Land Rights." *California Law Review* 63, no. 4: 848–885.

Lucas, Paul Nahoa. 1995. *A Dictionary of Hawaiian Legal Land-Terms.* Honolulu: Native Hawaiian Legal Corporation.

Lygate, J. M. 1915. "The Vanishing Kuleana." In *The Hawaiian Annual,* edited by Thos. G. Thrum. Honolulu: Thos. G. Thrum.

MacKenzie, Melody K., ed. 1991. *Native Hawaiian Rights Handbook.* Honolulu: Native Hawaiian Legal Corporation.

Malo, David. [1898] 1951. *Hawaiian Antiquities (Moolelo Hawaii).* Trans. Dr. Nathaniel B. Emerson, 1898. Honolulu: Bernice P. Museum Press.

McPherson, Michael M. 1991. "Trustees of Hawaiian Affairs v. Yamasaki and the Native Hawaiian Claim: Too Much of Nothing." *Environmental Law* 21: 453–497.

Menzies, Archibald. 1920. *Hawai'i Nei: 128 Years Ago.* Ed. W. H. Wilson. Honolulu: The New Freedom.

Merry, Sally Engle. 2000. *Colonizing Hawai'i: The Cultural Power of Law.* Princeton, N.J.: Princeton University Press.

Meyer, M. A. 2001. "Our Own Liberation: Reflections on Hawaiian Epistemology." *The Contemporary Pacific* 13, no. 1 (Spring): 124–148.

———. 1998a. "Native Hawaiian Epistemology: Contemporary Narratives." Ph.D. diss., Harvard Graduate School of Education.

———. 1998b. "Native Hawaiian Epistemology: Sites of Empowerment and Resistance." *Equity & Excellence in Education* 31, no. 1: 22–28.

———. 1998c. "Native Hawaiian Epistemology: Exploring Hawaiian Views of Knowledge." *Cultural Survival Quarterly* (Spring): 38–40.

Murakami, A. T., and B. Freitas. 1987. Native Hawaiian Claims Concerning Ocean Resources. Paper presented to the Hawai'i Ocean Affairs Conference, East-west Center, Honolulu.

Murton, Brian 1987. "Maori Territory." In *Southern Approaches: Geography in New Zealand,* edited by P. G. Holland. and W. B. Johnston. Christchurch: New Zealand Geographic Society (Inc.).

———. 1995. "A Fractured Land: Constructions of Knowledge about Land in Colonial New Zealand/Aotearoa." In *Proceedings of the 18th Conference,* New Zealand Geographical Society, University of Canterbury.

Nakuina, E. M. 1893. "Ancient Water Rights and Some of the Customs Pertaining to Them." In *The Hawaiian Annual,* edited by Thos. G. Thrum, 79–84. Honolulu: Thos. G. Thrum.

Pa Martin, E., and J. K. Burke. 1994. "Ocean Governance Strategies: Governance in Partnership with Na Keiki o Ke Kai, The Children of the Sea." Paper presented at the 28th Annual Conference of the Law of the Sea Institute, July 12.

Pawson, E. 1992. *Two New Zealands: Maori and European.* Ed. K. Anderson and Gale F. Wiley. New York: Halstead.

Pi'ianai'a, Ilima. n.d. "The Expression of Place in Hawaiian Folk Songs." Manuscript, University of Hawai'i.

Pukui, Mary Kawena. 1940. Transcription and translation out of Hawaiian-language newspaper *Ka Na'i Aupuni* June 16–18, 1906, from the files of Frances N. Frazier.

———. 1983. *'Ōlelo No'eau, Hawaiian Proverbs and Poetical Sayings.* Honolulu: Bernice P. Museum Press.

———, and S. H. Elbert. 1986. *Hawaiian Dictionary Revised and Enlarged Edition.* Honolulu: University of Hawai'i Press.

——, S. H. Elbert, and E. T. Moʻokini. 1976. *Place Names of Hawaiʻi*. 2nd ed. Honolulu. University of Hawaiʻi Press.

——, E. W. Haertig, and C. Lee. 1972. *Nana I Ke Kumu; Look to the Source*. Vols. I and II. Honolulu: Honolulu Hui Hānai, Queen Liliuʻokalani Children's Center.

——, and A. L. Korn. 1973. *The Echo of Our Song, Chants, and Poems of the Hawaiians*. Honolulu: University of Hawaiʻi Press.

Renwick, W. 1993. "Decolonising Ourselves from Within." Paper presented at the Waitangi Lecture Series, University of Edinburgh, April 13.

Rice, William Hyde. 1923. *Hawaiian Legends*. Honolulu: Bernice P. Bishop Museum Press bulletin 3.

Roberts, Helen. 1926. *Ancient Hawaiian Music*. Honolulu: Bernice P. Bishop Museum Press bulletin 29.

——. 1995. *Na Mele Welo Songs of our Heritage*. Honolulu: Bernice P. Bishop Museum Press.

Roberts, R. M. 1998. "Indigenous Knowledge and Western Science: Perspectives from the Pacific." In *Collected Papers No. 1*. Centre for Pacific Studies, University of Auckland.

——, and P. R. Wills. 1998. "Understanding Maori Epistemology, A Scientific Perspective." In *Tribal Epistemologies, Essays in the Philosophy of Anthropology*, edited by H. Wautischer. Aldershot, Brookfield, Singapore, and Sydney: Ashgate Press.

Schmitt, R. C. 1968. *Demographic Statistics of Hawaiʻi 1778–1965*. Honolulu: University of Hawaiʻi Press.

Silva, Noenoe. 2000. *Kanaka Maoli: Maluhia Me Ka Pono*. Honolulu: American Friends Service Community.

Stannard, David E. 1989. *Before the Horror: The Population of Hawaii on the Eve of Western Contact*. Honolulu: Social Science Research Institute, University of Hawaiʻi.

——. 1991. "Recounting the Fables of Savagery: Native Infanticide and the Functions of Political Myth." *Journal of American Studies* 25, no. 3: 381–418.

Stauffer, Robert H. 1989. "Land Tenure in Kahana, Hawaiʻi, 1846–1920." Ph.D. diss., University of Hawaiʻi.

Stokes, E. 1985. "Maori Research and Development." Discussion paper prepared for the Social Sciences Committee of the National Research Advisory Council.

Tava, Rerioterai, and Moses K. Keale. 1984. *Niihau, The Traditions of an Hawaiian Island*. Honolulu: Mutual Publishing Company.

Thrum, Thos. G., comp. and trans. 1910. *Hawaiian Traditions: Stories of the Menehune*. Chicago: A. C. McClurg & Co.

——. 1924. "Hawaiian Land Terms." In *The Hawaiian Annual*, edited by Thos. G. Thrum, 65-71. Honolulu: Thos. G. Thrum.

——. 1895. "Stories of the Menehune." In *The Hawaiian Annual*. Honolulu: Thos. G. Thrum.

Thurston, Lorrin A. 1904. *The Fundamental Law of Hawai'i.* Edited and indexed by Lorrin A. Thurston. Honolulu: Hawaiian Gazette Co.

Titcomb, Margaret. 1972. *Native Uses of Fish in Hawai'i.* Honolulu: University of Hawai'i Press.

Trask, Haunani K. 1993. *From a Native Daughter: Colonialism and Sovereignty in Hawai'i.* Monroe, Me.: Common Courage Press.

———. 1994. "Decolonizing Hawaiian Literature." Paper presented at the Pacific Literature Conference, Honolulu.

Tuan, Yi-Fu. 1971. "Man and Nature." Commission on College Geography Research Paper 10. Washington, D.C.: Association of American Geographers.

———. 1974. *Topophilia, A Study of Environmental Perception, Attitudes and Values.* Englewood Cliffs, N.J: Prentice Hall.

———. 1976. "Humanistic Geography." *Annals of the American Association of American Geographers* 66: 266–276.

———. 1977. *Space and Place.* Minneapolis: University of Minnesota Press.

———. 1991. "Language and the Making of Place: A Narrative-Descriptive Approach." *Annals of the American Association of Geographers* 81, no. 1: 684–696.

U.S. Board on Geographic Names. 1954. *Decisions on Names in Hawai'i: Cumulative Decision List No. 5403.* Washington, D.C.: U.S. Department of the Interior.

Waddell, E. 1997. "Thinking the Pacific: A Kanak View, as Expressed by Jean Marie Tjibaou." *Domodomo: A Scholarly Journal of the Fiji Museum* 11, no. 1.

Walker, Ranginui J. 1985. "Cultural Sensitivity to the Sanctity of Wananga (Knowledge)." Paper presented to the Archives & Records Association of New Zealand, July 9.

———. 1995. "Contestation of Power and Knowledge in the Politics of Culture." Keynote address, Twentieth Annual University of Hawai'i Pacific Islands Studies Conference, Honolulu, December 6–9.

Watson, L. J. 1932. "Old Hawaiian Land Huis—Their Development and Dissolution." Typescript.

Westervelt, William Drake. 1916. *Hawaiian Legends of Volcanoes Collected and Translated From the Hawaiian.* Boston and London. Facsimile of original edition of 1916 published by the University of Hawai'i Press.

———. 1922. "Kamehameha's Method of Government." *Hawaiian Historical Society Annual Report for 1921.* Honolulu.

Wichman, Frederick B. 1997. *More Kaua'i Tales.* Honolulu: Bamboo Ridge Press.

———. 1998. *Kaua'i: Ancient Place Names and Their Stories.* Honolulu: University of Hawai'i Press.

Whitney, Samuel, and William Richards. 1832. *He Hoikehonua: He Mea ia e Hoakaka'i i ke Ano Honua Nei, a me na Mea Maluna Iho.* O'ahu: Na Nā Misionari i Pa'i.

Yoon, Hong-Key. 1986. *Maori Mind, Maori Land: Essays on the Cultural Geography of the Maori People from an Outsider's Perspective.* New York: Berne.

YoungBear-Tibbetts, H. 1996. "The Struggle to Preserve Turangawaewae: Symbolic Discourse of Maori Political Activism." Ph.D. diss., University of Wisconsin.

Index

Note: Page numbers in italics refer to illustrations and captions.

About the Author

Carlos Andrade is a descendant of islanders of both the Atlantic and Pacific oceans. He lives on Kaua'i, the northernmost of the inhabited Hawaiian Islands, where some of his ancestors have lived for close to two thousand years. His other ancestors came from the Madeira Islands off the coast of Africa and Portugal. A father of three and grandfather of four, he has lived as a subsistence farmer/fisherman, and worked as a musician, boat captain, and construction worker. He is a composer of songs and a writer and teller of stories. He returned to university in his mid-forties to earn a bachelor of arts in Hawaiian Studies (1989), a master of education (1993), and a doctorate in geography (2001). Dr. Andrade served as a crewmember on the voyaging canoe *Hōkūle'a* on voyages from Aotearoa to Tonga and Samoa (1985) and from Rarotonga to Tahiti and Hawai'i (1993). He is now a professor at Kamakakūokalani Center for Hawaiian Studies at the University of Hawai'i at Mānoa, dividing his time between teaching classes about traditional navigation, Hawaiian astronomy, and resource management; cultivating family *kuleana* on Kaua'i; composing *mele;* playing *kī hō'alu;* building and sailing canoes; surfing the waves of Kaua'i; mapping ancestral lands; and working with elders in the Native Hawaiian community.

Small graphics of Makana, throughout,
courtesy of Maile Andrade

Cover and interior design and composition by Barbara Pope Book Design
Text in Minion and Brioso, display type in Brioso and Charlemagne
Printed on 70# Finch Opaque Cream White Smooth, 416 ppi